Editor

Erica N. Russikoff, M.A.

Illustrator

Clint McKnight

Cover Artist

Brenda DiAntonis

Editor in Chief

Karen J. Goldfluss, M.S. Ed.

Imaging

Rosa C. See

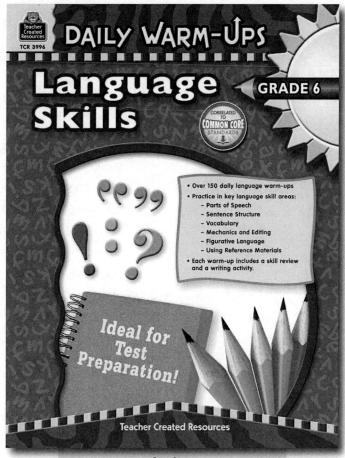

Author

Mary Rosenberg

Publisher

Mary D. Smith, M.S. Ed.

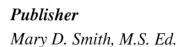

Correlations to the Common Core State Standards can be found at *http://www.teachercreated.com/standards/*.

Teacher Created Resources, Inc.

12621 Western Avenue

Garden Grove, CA 92841

www.teachercreated.com

ISBN: 978-1-4206-3996-4

©2009 Teacher Created Resources,
Reprinted, 2017

Made in U.S.A.

Teacher Created Resources

TABLE OF CONTENTS

INTRODUCTION

Welcome to Teacher Created Resources' *Daily Warm-Ups: Language Skills* for Grade 6. In each book of the *Daily Warm-Ups* series, there are over 150 Warm-Ups that cover a wide range of writing skills: grammar, parts of speech, vocabulary, punctuation, and mechanics. Each Warm-Up provides a brief overview of a particular skill, an example of using the skill correctly, an activity for the skill, as well as a follow-up writing activity for applying the skill.

In the *Daily Warm-Ups* series, the Table of Contents, the Standards Correlation, and the Tracking Sheet are all useful tools. The Table of Contents and the Standards Correlation allow you to pinpoint specific skills for the student to work on. The Standards Correlation shows the general skills that a student or child should know at each grade level. Additionally, the Tracking Sheet allows you and/or the student to keep track of his or her progress.

Daily Warm-Ups are ideal for both parents and teachers and are easy to use. For parents, select the skill you want to work on with your child, tear out the page, and preview the material with your child. Be sure to have your child note the topic that is being covered. This will allow your child to access the knowledge and information that he or she already knows about the skill. Continue to go over the page with your child, so the child will know what to do. When your child has completed the page, take a few minutes to correct the work and address any errors your child made. An easy-to-use answer key starts on page 164.

For the classroom teacher, simply identify the skill page that you want to use with the students, and photocopy a class set. If several pages are available on a specific skill, you might want to photocopy the pages into individual packets for each student. When presenting the page to your students, start at the top of the page where it notes the topic (skill) that is being covered. By doing this, the students will begin to access the prior knowledge and information they already know about the topic. Immediately following the topic will be a brief definition of the topic. Have your students read it, so they can apply this knowledge in the Practice section. The Practice section has the students independently (or with guided practice) apply the skill. The final section, Write On!, provides a writing activity that incorporates that page's specific skill.

The skills covered in *Daily Warm-Ups: Language Skills* are skills that are used and needed every day. Help your children or students master these skills, as they will use these skills throughout the rest of their educational careers and lives.

STANDARDS CORRELATION

Each lesson in *Daily Warm-Ups: Language Skills* for Grade 6 meets one or more of the following language arts standards, which are used with permission from McREL (Copyright 2009 McREL. Mid-continent Research for Education and Learning. 4601 DTC Boulevard, Suite 500, Denver, CO 80237. Telephone: 303-337-0990. Web site: *www.mcrel.org/standards-benchmarks*.) Visit *http://www.teachercreated.com/standards* for correlations to the Common Core State Standards.

Standard 1: Uses the general skills and strategies of the writing process

• Uses a variety of prewriting strategies	Pages: 70–73
• Uses a variety of strategies to draft and revise written work	Page: 16
• Uses a variety of strategies to edit and publish written work	Pages: 136–152, 155–159, 162–163
• Uses content, style, and structure appropriate for specific audiences and purposes	Pages: 8, 70–75
• Writes expository compositions	Pages: 31, 70–73, 75
• Writes compositions about autobiographical incidents	Page: 73
• Writes compositions that address problems/solutions	Pages: 31, 72

Standard 2: Uses the stylistic and rhetorical aspects of writing

• Uses descriptive language that clarifies and enhances ideas	Pages: 37–46
• Uses paragraph form in writing	Pages: 71–73, 75
• Uses a variety of sentence structures to expand and embed ideas	Pages: 62–67
• Uses explicit transitional devices	Pages: 70–73

Standard 3: Uses grammatical and mechanical conventions in written compositions

• Uses pronouns in written compositions	Pages: 8–21
• Uses nouns in written compositions	Pages: 22–29
• Uses verbs in written compositions	Pages: 30–36
• Uses adjectives in written compositions	Pages: 37–46
• Uses adverbs in written compositions	Pages: 47–51
• Uses prepositions and coordinating conjunctions in written compositions	Pages: 52–60
• Uses interjections in written compositions	Page: 61

STANDARDS CORRELATION

Standard 3: Uses grammatical and mechanical conventions in written compositions *(cont.)*

- Uses conventions of spelling in written compositions   Pages: 76–102, 155–159

- Uses conventions of capitalization in written compositions   Pages: 62, 148–152

- Uses conventions of punctuation in written compositions   Pages: 62, 136–147

- Uses appropriate format in written compositions   Pages: 134–135

Standard 4: Gathers and uses information for research purposes

- Uses library catalogs and periodical indexes to locate sources for research topics   Page: 130

- Uses a variety of resources to gather information for research topics   Pages: 132–133

- Uses appropriate methods to cite and document reference sources   Pages: 133–135

Standard 5: Uses the general skills and strategies of the reading process

- Uses word origins and derivations to understand word meaning   Pages: 76–86

- Uses a variety of strategies to extend reading vocabulary   Pages: 90–117

Standard 7: Uses reading skills and strategies to understand and interpret a variety of informational texts

- Knows the defining characteristics of a variety of informational texts   Pages: 118–133

TRACKING SHEET

Parts of Speech		Parts of Speech *(cont.)*		Parts of Speech *(cont.)*		Sentence Structure		Vocabulary	
Page 8		Page 26		Page 44		Page 62		Page 76	
Page 9		Page 27		Page 45		Page 63		Page 77	
Page 10		Page 28		Page 46		Page 64		Page 78	
Page 11		Page 29		Page 47		Page 65		Page 79	
Page 12		Page 30		Page 48		Page 66		Page 80	
Page 13		Page 31		Page 49		Page 67		Page 81	
Page 14		Page 32		Page 50		Page 68		Page 82	
Page 15		Page 33		Page 51		Page 69		Page 83	
Page 16		Page 34		Page 52		Page 70		Page 84	
Page 17		Page 35		Page 53		Page 71		Page 85	
Page 18		Page 36		Page 54		Page 72		Page 86	
Page 19		Page 37		Page 55		Page 73		Page 87	
Page 20		Page 38		Page 56		Page 74		Page 88	
Page 21		Page 39		Page 57		Page 75		Page 89	
Page 22		Page 40		Page 58				Page 90	
Page 23		Page 41		Page 59				Page 91	
Page 24		Page 42		Page 60				Page 92	
Page 25		Page 43		Page 61				Page 93	

Vocabulary *(cont.)*		Figurative Language		Reference Materials		Punctuation		Mechanics and Editing	
Page 94		Page 108		Page 118		Page 136		Page 148	
Page 95		Page 109		Page 119		Page 137		Page 149	
Page 96		Page 110		Page 120		Page 138		Page 150	
Page 97		Page 111		Page 121		Page 139		Page 151	
Page 98		Page 112		Page 122		Page 140		Page 152	
Page 99		Page 113		Page 123		Page 141		Page 153	
Page 100		Page 114		Page 124		Page 142		Page 154	
Page 101		Page 115		Page 125		Page 143		Page 155	
Page 102		Page 116		Page 126		Page 144		Page 156	
Page 103		Page 117		Page 127		Page 145		Page 157	
Page 104				Page 128		Page 146		Page 158	
Page 105				Page 129		Page 147		Page 159	
Page 106				Page 130				Page 160	
Page 107				Page 131				Page 161	
				Page 132				Page 162	
				Page 133				Page 163	
				Page 134					
				Page 135					

DAILY WARM-UPS

Name _____ Date _____

Personal Pronouns

A **pronoun** can replace a noun—a person, place, thing, or idea—in a sentence. A personal pronoun can be identified by its "person."

- *First person* refers to the speaker or the writer. The personal pronouns used are *I* or *we*.
- *Second person* refers to the person or people being spoken to or written to. The personal pronoun used is *you* for both one person and more than one person.
- *Third person* refers to the person or people being talked about or written about. The personal pronouns used are *he, she, it,* and *they*.

PRACTICE

Identify the "person" used in each paragraph.

Paragraph #1

When I was young, my best friend and I enjoyed skipping rocks. We would walk down to Miller's Pond and look for smooth, flat rocks. When we found the perfect rocks, we would take turns skipping the rocks across the pond. Once, I even skipped a rock fifteen times. My friend skipped one rock eighteen times! It was a fun way to spend an afternoon.

Person:_____

Paragraph #2

Sisters and brothers are such pains! They are always getting into stuff and causing problems. Sisters leave their dolls and play clothes on the living room carpet. Brothers leave their toy trucks and toy soldiers under the blankets and all over the front lawn. Sisters and brothers are so messy!

Person:_____

Paragraph #3

Getting an education is one of the most important things you can do. Research shows that the more education you receive, the more money you will earn over your lifetime. The best thing that you can do is to stay in school, graduate from a college or a trade school, and earn a good living to support yourself and your family.

Person:_____

WRITE ON!

On a separate sheet of paper, write a paragraph in either the first, second, or third person. Exchange papers with a classmate. Ask the classmate to read the paragraph and identify the person used in the paragraph.

Name _____   Date _____

Subject Pronouns

A **subject pronoun** can replace the subject's noun—a person, place, thing, or idea—in a sentence.

    Example: *Riley* is going to the dance.

                 She is going to the dance.

Singular	Plural
I	We
You	You
He, She, It	They

PRACTICE

Write an appropriate subject pronoun on each line.

1. fire engine _____
2. the Dalmatian _____
3. Fido _____
4. the firefighters _____
5. Mrs. Hightower _____

6. the fire chief and I _____
7. the building _____
8. Captain Pete _____
9. referring to oneself _____
10. all units _____

Write an appropriate subject pronoun for the underlined word(s).

    Example: <u>The firefighters</u> raced to put out the fire.   <u>They</u>

1. <u>The news anchor</u> was covering the latest fire. _____
2. <u>The fire chief</u> thought it might be arson. _____
3. <u>Many people</u> almost lost their lives. _____
4. <u>Marsha</u> lost her home during one of the fires. _____
5. <u>Franklin</u> saved many lives. _____
6. Upon smelling smoke and seeing flames, <u>Franklin</u> called 911. _____
7. <u>Franklin</u> immediately called the fire department. _____
8. <u>Everyone</u> got out of the apartment building safely. _____
9. <u>The apartment manager</u> called Franklin a hero. _____
10. <u>All of Franklin's teachers and friends</u> were proud of him. _____

WRITE ON!

On a separate sheet of paper, write a paragraph on a topic of your choice. Use subject pronouns in the paragraph, and underline them.

Name _____   Date _____

Subject Pronouns

A **subject pronoun** can replace the subject's noun—a person, place, thing, or idea—in a sentence.

Example: *Alice* loves to work in the garden.

She loves to work in the garden.

Singular	Plural
I	We
You	You
He, She, It	They

PRACTICE

Draw a line under the subject's noun(s). Write an appropriate subject pronoun on the line.

Example: <u>Dr. Fucaloro</u> likes teaching her French class.   She

1. Where is Mrs. Greenstone?   _____

2. Rover loves to sleep in front of the fireplace.   _____

3. Stella, Jim, and I are on the cheer team.   _____

4. Dean and Stacy finished building the miniature dollhouse.   _____

5. Mom and Dad are going to the symphony tonight.   _____

6. Recycle-R-Us and Eco-Green are two local recycling companies.   _____

7. Homework is overflowing from my backpack.   _____

8. Ken cleaned the air conditioner's filter.   _____

9. Trees help keep the air clean.   _____

10. Parents are important people.   _____

11. Doug needs to remember to stop at the stop signs.   _____

12. Grace, Bea, and Maggie are neighborhood friends.   _____

Write a sentence using each of the following subject pronouns.

1. you (singular): _____

2. you (plural): _____

WRITE ON!

What problem might you run into if you only used subject pronouns when writing a paragraph? Write your response on a separate sheet of paper.

Name _____   Date _____

Object Pronouns

An **object pronoun** receives the action from the verb. The object noun can be replaced with an appropriate object pronoun.

Example: Lanny gave the book to *Matt*.

Lanny gave the book to *him*.

Singular	Plural
me	us
you	you
him, her, it	them

PRACTICE

Underline each common or proper noun that can be replaced with an object pronoun and still maintain the clarity of the sentence. Write the object pronoun above the noun.

Ralph, Sue, and I went to eat lunch at The Burger Joint. At The Burger Joint, all three of us looked at the menu. The Burger Joint offered over thirty different kinds of hamburgers with every kind of topping available. After examining the menu, Ralph decided to take the plunge. Ralph ordered the giant hamburger deluxe with everything on it. The hamburger was three pounds of cooked meat with tomatoes, lettuce, bacon, cheese, special sauce, onions, and pickles. Whenever this special hamburger was ordered, a large cow bell was rung. When the hamburger was brought to Ralph, he took a big bite of the juicy burger. Ralph turned to Sue and me and said, "Wow! This is the best burger ever!"

Sue and I decided to order a giant hamburger deluxe with everything on it, too. When it was brought to Sue and me, we told the waiters, "Thanks! We can't wait to eat it all!" Sue tried her best, but she still had a lot of her burger left. So, the waiter brought Sue a doggie bag to take the left-over burger home. Ralph, Sue, and I left the waiters a big tip. We can't wait to go back to The Burger Joint again.

WRITE ON!

What makes a hamburger delicious? On a separate sheet of paper, describe the best burger you have ever had. Use object pronouns in the paragraph, and underline them.

Name _____   Date _____

Possessive Adjectives and Possessive Pronouns

A **possessive pronoun** shows ownership and takes the place of a noun. Therefore, it is not immediately followed by a noun and can stand alone.

Example: This backpack is *mine*.

Singular	Plural
mine	ours
yours	yours
his, hers	theirs

A **possessive adjective** shows ownership but is immediately followed by a noun. It cannot stand alone.

Example: This is *my* backpack.

Singular	Plural
my	our
your	your
his, her, its	their

PRACTICE

Rewrite each sentence using a possessive pronoun or a possessive adjective.

Example: The book belongs to Corinne.

It is her book. *or* The book is hers.

1. That is Franklin and Gloria's house.

    _____

2. The school we attend is over a hundred years old.

    _____

3. Lindsey's collage is full of photographs and cards.

    _____

4. That is Phil's television.

    _____

5. This laptop is Dr. Pilgreen's.

    _____

WRITE ON!

On a separate sheet of paper, describe something you made and how you made it. It could be something as simple as a paper airplane or elaborate as a bridge made out of toothpicks. Use possessive pronouns in the paragraph, and underline them.

Name _____   Date _____

Pronouns Agree with the Antecedent

A **pronoun** can refer to something earlier in the text, called the antecedent. The pronoun and its antecedent must agree in:

- **number**—either singular or plural

Singular Pronouns	Plural Pronouns
I	I
You	You
He, She, It	They

- **gender**—either male or female

Male Pronouns	Female Pronouns
He	She

- **person**—either first, second, or third

Person	Pronoun
First	I
Second	You
Third	He, She, It, They

PRACTICE

Underline and identify the pronoun-antecedent agreement problem in each sentence.

Example: <u>Jenna</u> used <u>his</u> grandmother's recipe.

Problem: No gender agreement. Jenna is not a "he."

1. Fred, Willard, and Jim must see his teacher after school.

   Problem: _____

2. If you go surfing, she needs to be on the lookout for sharks.

   Problem: _____

3. Raphael and Roberta run every day, and we lift weight several times per week.

   Problem: _____

4. Keith designs shirts, and she is very good at it.

   Problem: _____

5. Enid repainted the cabinets, and they refinished the floors.

   Problem: _____

WRITE ON!

On a separate sheet of paper, write four sentences with pronoun-antecedent agreement problems.
Exchange papers with a classmate. Ask the classmate to rewrite the sentences correctly.

Name _____ Date _____

Indefinite Pronouns

An **indefinite pronoun** does not take the place of another noun. Instead, an indefinite pronoun acts as a noun. Most indefinite pronouns are singular and require a singular verb.

Example: *Everyone* that studied did well on the test.

Common Indefinite Pronouns

anybody	everybody	no one	somebody
anyone	everyone	nobody	someone
anything	everything	nothing	something

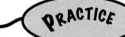

Write sentences using indefinite pronouns.

Example: Everybody is excited about summer vacation.

1. _____
2. _____
3. _____
4. _____
5. _____
6. _____
7. _____
8. _____
9. _____
10. _____

Circle the mistakes in the Weekly Bulletin.

Everybody are going to the assembly on Friday. Each and every person is expected to sit quietly

on the chairs. Anybody not doing this will be sent to the office. Everyone will clap at the end of

each song. Nobody are stamping feet on the floor or banging fists on the tables. Does anyone has

any questions?

On a separate sheet of paper, write a bulletin detailing the events that will happen this week at your school. The events can be real or made-up. Use indefinite pronouns in the paragraph, and underline them. Check to make sure the correct form of the verb follows each indefinite pronoun.

Name _____ Date _____

Indefinite Pronouns

An **indefinite pronoun** replaces a noun in a sentence. The noun it replaces is not specified.

> Example: *One* of the boys gave up his ticket.
>
> *One* is the indefinite pronoun. It refers to *his*.

- With a singular indefinite pronoun, use a singular verb and singular pronouns.
  Example: Does *anybody want* another piece of cake?

- With a plural indefinite pronoun, use a plural verb and plural pronouns.
  Example: A *few were* asking for tickets to the school play.

- For indefinite pronouns that can be singular or plural, it depends upon what the indefinite pronoun refers to.
  Example: *All* of the kids sat on their chairs. *All* of the newspaper was wet.

Singular Indefinite Pronouns			Plural Indefinite Pronouns	Singular or Plural Indefinite Pronouns
another	everybody	nothing	both	all
anybody	everyone	one	(a) few	any
anyone	everything	other	many	more
anything	neither	somebody	others	most
each	nobody	someone	several	none
either	no one	something		some

PRACTICE

Add an indefinite pronoun to each sentence.

1. _____ left a jacket on the couch.

2. Is there _____ wrong?

3. _____ have left their lunch pails in the classroom.

4. _____ students are graduating with high honors.

5. _____ of my puppies is missing!

6. _____ cheerleaders have their pompoms ready.

7. _____ team is ready to do its routine.

8. _____ people are going on the trip to Mexico.

WRITE ON!

On a separate sheet of paper, tell about something you have done with a team or with a group. Use indefinite pronouns in the paragraph, and underline them.

Name _____   Date _____

Intensive Pronouns

An **intensive pronoun** ends in *–self* (or *–selves*) and emphasizes the noun or pronoun. It also immediately follows the noun or pronoun in a sentence.

Example: *She, herself*, made the bridge out of bottle caps.

Subject Pronouns	
Singular	**Plural**
I	We
You	You
He, She, It	They
One	

Intensive Pronouns	
Singular	**Plural**
myself	ourselves
yourself	yourselves
himself, herself, itself	themselves
oneself	

PRACTICE

Use several subject pronouns and intensive pronouns in sentences.

Example: I, myself, painted the entire house.

1. _____

2. _____

3. _____

Underline the intensive pronouns used in the paragraph.

You are not going to believe what I did! I, myself, actually built a miniature log cabin using pretzels. It was for my American History class, which is taught by Mr. Rogers. Mr. Rogers, himself, was so impressed with my pretzel log cabin that he said it should be put in the Smithsonian Museum! My parents were so proud of me. And, I have to admit, I, myself, was proud of me, too!

Rewrite the above paragraph without the intensive pronouns.

_____

_____

_____

_____

_____

WRITE ON!

On a separate sheet of paper, write about something you achieved or did all by yourself. Use intensive pronouns in the paragraph, and underline them.

Name _____   Date _____

Reflexive Pronouns

A **reflexive pronoun** is similar to an intensive pronoun. The main difference is the location of the pronoun. For reflexive pronouns, the subject and the object are the same person.

Example: *I made it myself.*

Subject Pronouns

Singular	Plural
I	We
You	You
He, She, It	They
One	

Reflexive Pronouns

Singular	Plural
myself	ourselves
yourself	yourselves
himself, herself, itself	themselves
oneself	

PRACTICE

Use several subject pronouns and reflexives pronouns in sentences.

Example: She drew the house plans herself.

1. _____

2. _____

3. _____

4. _____

5. _____

Underline the reflexive pronouns used in the paragraph.

Our school holds a carnival each year. The students help get everything ready. Ted is in charge of making signs. He painted all of the booth signs himself. The signs looked great. Marge and Madge are in charge of ticket sales. They outdid themselves this year. They sold more tickets than anyone ever had before. I am in charge of refreshments. I made a flyer and sent it home with all of the students. I was able to get over five hundred cases of soda donated to the carnival. I was very proud of myself.

WRITE ON!

Does your school have a carnival? Have you ever been to a carnival? Write about the experience on a separate sheet of paper. Use reflexive pronouns in the paragraph, and underline them.

Name _____ Date _____

Demonstrative Pronouns

Demonstrative pronouns identify or point to nouns. Demonstrative pronouns refer to people, places, things, or ideas. Demonstrative pronouns are *this, that, these,* and *those.*

    Example: Students loitering after school will be given detention.

              Those loitering after school will be given detention.

Some demonstrative pronouns show distance or indicate one item.

- Use *this* for something that is nearby.   Example: *This* is my coat.
- Use *that* for something farther away.   Example: *That* (pointing across the room) is your coat.

Some demonstrative pronouns indicate time or more than one item.

- Use *these* to indicate now or things that are nearby.   Example: *These* are for you.
- Use *those* to indicate the present or past or   Example: *Those* are for you.
  things that are farther away.   *Those* were for you.

 PRACTICE

Rewrite each sentence replacing the noun with a demonstrative pronoun.

(that   these   this   those)

    Example: The cookies are delicious.

           These are delicious.

1. The sandwich tastes awful! (Sandwich is in front of you.)

    _____

2. The books are for you. (Books are in your hands.)

    _____

3. The grades are fantastic! (You are looking at your report card.)

    _____

4. The toaster is an incredible invention. (The toaster is in another room.)

    _____

5. The earrings belonged to my grandmother. (Earrings are across the room.)

    _____

 **WRITE ON!**

On a separate sheet of paper, write four sentences. Use a demonstrative pronoun in each sentence.

Name _____   Date _____

Relative Pronouns

A **relative pronoun** is used to join a dependent clause (a group of related words with a subject and a verb that cannot stand alone) with an independent clause (a group of related words with a subject and a verb that can stand alone). The result is a complex sentence. The relative pronoun can be either the subject or the object of the dependent clause.

Example: Mrs. Swank, *who* is a wonderful party planner, prepared the buffet.

When referring to people, use *who, whom, whoever,* or *whomever.*

• Use *who* or *whoever* when referring to the subject of the sentence.

• Use *whom* or *whomever* when referring to the object of the sentence.

Complete each sentence with the correct relative pronoun.

Example: Mr. Harwell, <u>who</u> designed his own house, is an architect.

1. Fatima, _____ is always talking up a storm, was quiet during the performance.

2. Toros and _____ he was with at lunchtime were helpful in the cafeteria.

3. The package is for James and _____ he is working with.

4. Marilyn has a little sister, _____ she takes care of all of the time.

5. Women _____ are stay-at-home moms work just as hard as women who work outside of the home.

6. My two brothers, _____ I love very much, also drive me crazy!

7. Mr. Tickler and the mad-scientist inventor, with _____ he has worked for more than twenty years, have created a new use for bubble gum.

8. The pilot, _____ was assisted by the copilot, landed the aircraft safely.

9. The blonde-haired baby, _____ Joseph was carrying in a baby backpack, gurgled and chortled quite happily.

10. Grandpa Dix and his favorite granddaughter, _____ he takes fishing each summer, can always be found sitting on the front porch.

On a separate sheet of paper, write five sentences using relative pronouns. Underline the relative pronoun used in each sentence.

Name _____   Date _____

Relative Pronouns

A **relative pronoun** is used to join a dependent clause (a group of related words with a subject and a verb that cannot stand alone) with an independent clause (a group of related words with a subject and a verb that can stand alone). The result is a complex sentence. The relative pronoun can be either the subject or the object of the dependent clause.

Example: The package *that* was left on the porch was large and heavy.

When referring to places, things, or ideas, use *which, that,* or *whatever.*

- Use *which* (with a comma) when referring to the subject or object of the sentence.

- Use *which* when the information is not critical to the understanding of the sentence.

- Use *that* when referring to the subject or object of the sentence.

- Use *that* when the information is important to the understanding of the sentence.

- Use *whatever* (with a comma) when referring to more than one place, thing, or idea.

PRACTICE

Complete each sentence with the correct relative pronoun.

Example: Karen's plan, <u>which</u> might work, will require a lot of resources.

1. The homemade quilt _____ Grandma made is a family heirloom.

2. The home office, _____ doubles as a toy room, is very cluttered.

3. The jet _____ is owned by Lady and Lord Maxwell is kept at the Preston Airport.

4. The jeans, _____ are in different sizes, are perfect for the yard sale.

5. Roller skates or roller blades, _____ they are called, are still dangerous shoes.

6. The mansion _____ is on the corner of Nob Hill and Tiffany Avenue is over 200 years old.

Write two sentences. Use a relative pronoun in each sentence. Add commas if necessary.

1. _____

2. _____

WRITE ON!

On a separate sheet of paper, write a paragraph on a topic of your choice. Use relative pronouns in the paragraph, and underline them. Check to make sure commas were used, if necessary.

Name _____   Date _____

Interrogative Pronouns

Interrogative pronouns introduce questions. Interrogative pronouns are *what, which, who, whom,* and *whose.*

    Example: *Whose* jacket is this?

Write a question for each answer using an interrogative pronoun.

    Example: Liza likes to make lasagna, panini, and tiramisu.
              What kinds of food does Liza like to make?

1. It is Taylor's lunch money.

   _____

2. I will take the chocolate cupcake with sprinkles on top.

   _____

3. Bob was knocking at the door.

   _____

4. The package was for Aunt Lucy.

   _____

5. Professor Geary wanted to know who was attending the graduation ceremony.

   _____

6. The Nelsons have been to Seattle, Washington, many times.

   _____

7. Jan's bike is blocking the driveway.

   _____

8. We will have pizza and salad for dinner tonight.

   _____

9. The coach likes the blue and silver uniforms best.

   _____

10. The gift is for Grandma and Grandpa's fiftieth anniversary.

   _____

On a separate sheet of paper, write a question for each interrogative pronoun. Exchange papers with a classmate. Ask the classmate to answer each question.

Name _____   Date _____

Possessive Nouns

A **noun** names a person, place, thing, or idea.

　　Examples: actor, studio, set, fame

A **proper noun** names a specific person, place, thing, or idea. A proper noun begins with a capital letter.

　　Examples: Jackie Starlet, Hollywood, *On the Lot* (a movie)

A **possessive noun** shows ownership.

　　Example: *Jackie Starlet's* character in *On the Lot* was very believable.

　• To make a singular noun possessive, add an apostrophe –s ('*s*) to the end of the noun.
　　Example: John's truck

　• If the singular noun ends in an –s, you can just add an apostrophe to the end of the noun. You can also add an apostrophe –s ('*s*) to the end of the noun. Whatever you decide, be consistent.
　　Example: The dress' hem　　　　　　Example: My boss's bookmark

PRACTICE

Rewrite each sentence using a possessive noun.

　　Example: Zoe has a new car seat.

　　　　　　 Zoe's car seat is new.

1. The seamstress has many different and bright thread colors.

　　_____

2. The hat of the sailor flew overboard.

　　_____

3. The testimony of the witness rang true.

　　_____

4. Eli has an older brother who is in eighth grade.

　　_____

5. The project of the class was to write reports on insects.

　　_____

WRITE ON!

Which possessive rule surprised you? Why? Write your response on a separate sheet of paper.

Name _____   Date _____

Possessive Nouns

A **noun** names a person, place, thing, or idea.

    Examples: teacher, classroom, backpack, knowledge

A **proper noun** names a specific person, place, thing, or idea. A proper noun begins with a capital letter.

    Examples: Ms. Smith, Silverleaf High School, *American History* (a book)

A **possessive noun** shows ownership.

    Example: Ms. Smith's class at Silverleaf High School is reading about Pocahontas.

- To make a singular proper noun that ends in –*s* possessive, add an apostrophe to the end of the noun. You can also add an apostrophe –*s* (*'s*) to the end of the noun. Whatever you decide, be consistent.

    Example: Charles' sour lemons   Example: Charles's sour lemons

- If a plural noun ends in –*s*, add an apostrophe to the end of the noun.

    Example: the girls' restroom

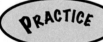

Rewrite each sentence using a possessive noun.

    Example: The restroom of the boys is always filled with trash.

             The boys' restroom is always filled with trash.

1. The marbles that belonged to Kris fell down onto the classroom floor.

    _____

2. The paperwork is important and it belongs to Mr. Veen.

    _____

3. The meeting for the principals was held in the school library.

    _____

4. The doors of the lockers were in need of repair.

    _____

5. The signs for Lucas were made by his parents.

    _____

On a separate sheet of paper, write four sentences that fit the two possessive rules covered on this page.

Name _____   Date _____

Possessive Nouns

A **noun** names a person, place, thing, or idea.

Examples: parent, home, mailbox, love

A **proper noun** names a specific person, place, thing, or idea. A proper noun begins with a capital letter.

Examples: Grandpa Bert, Trickling Creek Drive, Oreo (the dog)

A **possessive noun** shows ownership.

Example: We spent the weekend at Grandpa Bert's house on Trickling Creek Drive.

• If a plural noun does not end in –*s*, add an apostrophe –*s* (*'s*).

Example: children's story time

• If there is joint ownership (possession), make the noun closest to the item owned possessive.

Example: Lisa and Sue's project

Rewrite each sentence using a possessive noun.

Example: The toys of Gracie and Bea are always covered in dirt and spit!

Gracie and Bea's toys are always covered in dirt and spit!

1. The room of Bill and Will is always spotless.

   _____

2. The feathers of the geese flew all around the sky before dropping to the ground.

   _____

3. The homes of the mice were made in the walls of the house.

   _____

4. The paint on the ceiling and door was cracked and peeling.

   _____

5. The handles on the pot and pan were made of walnut.

   _____

6. The votes of the people were counted by hand.

   _____

On a separate sheet of paper and following the two rules presented on this page, write four sentences for a classmate to correct.

Name _____   Date _____

Possessive Nouns

A **noun** names a person, place, thing, or idea.

    Examples: president, office, plane, freedom

A **proper noun** names a specific person, place, thing, or idea. A proper noun begins with a capital letter.

    Examples: President Obama, Oval Office, *Air Force One* (a plane)

A **possessive noun** shows ownership.

    Example: President Obama's flight was swift aboard *Air Force One*.

    • If there is separate ownership, each noun is possessive.
    Example: Jake's and John's reports on the United States government were excellent.

    • For compound nouns, use the correct possessive form for the word closest to the item owned.
    Example: The commander-in-chief's kids ran into his office.

Rewrite each sentence using a possessive noun(s).

    Example: The lies of Vincent and Gabriel are always getting them into trouble.

              Vincent's and Gabriel's lies are always getting them into trouble.

1. The injuries of Sean and Deandre kept the team from winning the championship.

    _____

2. The declaration of the chairman of the board settled the argument.

    _____

3. The scores of Rosa and Gabe were the best and the worst in the class.

    _____

4. The business of my brother-in-law is doing well.

    _____

5. The inventions of Teddy and Franklin have helped people from many different generations.

    _____

On a separate sheet of paper, write a paragraph on a topic of your choice. Use possessive nouns, and underline them. Check to make sure you followed the rules of possession.

Name _____   Date _____

Irregular Plural Nouns

Most **nouns** add an –s or –es to show more than one.

> Examples: Heather has a hammer.   Heather has two hammers.
>
> Ralph found a box.   Ralph found several boxes.

Some nouns are **irregular.** They do not add an –s or –es to show more than one. Instead, the noun changes form.

> Example: The *man* couldn't move the heavy car.
>
> The ten *men* could move the heavy car.

PRACTICE

Write the plural form for each irregular noun.

> Example: goose _____geese_____

1. foot _____   4. woman _____

2. mouse _____   5. ox _____

3. die _____   6. tooth _____

Circle the mistake in each sentence. Write the correct word on the line.

> Example: My (foots) hurt!   _____feet_____

1. The mans were moving the heavy equipment.   _____

2. Did the womans have any questions?   _____

3. One children ordered books from the book order. _____

Draw a line through the mistakes in the paragraph. Write the correct word above the line.

My family and I were playing a game called "Catch an Oxen." We each picked a token. My brother was a mice. My dad was a dog. My mom was a bird, and I was a cat. We each put our token in the start box. On the first roll of the dice, I moved ahead three spaces and landed in the space that said, "Lost a teeth, move back two spaces." My brother went next. He landed in the space that said, "Fell out of a tree and broke your leg in halves. Go back to Start." So far, the game wasn't off to a great start.

WRITE ON!

On a separate sheet of paper, tell about a favorite game and how the game is played. Use irregular plural nouns, and underline them. Share the paragraph with a classmate.

Name _____ Date _____

Irregular Plural Nouns

Most **nouns** add an –*s* or –*es* to show more than one.

Examples: Rich has one cat.   Rich has many cats.

Mary bought one dress.   Mary bought two dresses.

Some nouns are **irregular.** Some nouns do not add an –*s* or even change form when they name more than one item. Instead, the noun stays the same, and the context, or the surrounding words, help determine if the noun is singular or plural.

PRACTICE

Decide whether the underlined noun is singular or plural.

Example: Seth saw a <u>bison</u> wandering on the open range.   _____singular_____

1. The Native Americans used hides of <u>deer</u> for homes and clothing.   _____

2. The school mascot is the <u>moose</u>.   _____

3. Mary's little lamb will grow up to become a <u>sheep</u>.   _____

4. The <u>swine</u> are out wallowing in the mud.   _____

5. At the zoo, we saw three <u>bison</u> chewing on grass.   _____

6. Pete raised a <u>swine</u> for the country market.   _____

7. The <u>moose</u> are stampeding into town scaring all of the local folks.   _____

8. Five <u>sheep</u> ate all of the grass in Mrs. Johnson's backyard.   _____

Which clue words tell you that the noun is singular?

_____

_____

Which clue words tell you that the noun is plural?

_____

_____

WRITE ON!

Select one of the animals from above. On a separate sheet of paper, write all of the facts that you know about that particular animal. Underline the clue words in each sentence that identify the noun as being singular or plural.

Name _____   Date _____

DAILY Warm-Up 21

Irregular Plural Nouns

Some **nouns** stay the same in singular and plural form, or an *–s* or *–es* can be added to make the noun plural.

    Example: I caught one *cod* while fishing with Grandma.

              Grandma caught a dozen *cod*.

              Grandma caught many *cods*.

PRACTICE

Write the singular and/or plural forms for each noun.

Singular	Plural	Plural (adding *–s* or *–es*)
Example: elk	elk	elks
1.	quail	
2.		grouses
3.	flounder	
4.	salmon	
5. shrimp		
6. fish		
7.	herring	
8.		trouts

Read the story. Underline the irregular plural nouns.

My family and I spent a week at our cabin in the woods. Each morning, we would start the day with a hike along the different paths and trails. One morning, we saw the tracks from elk! We could tell by the different sizes of the tracks that the elk might have been a family. It was exciting. Then, my family and I followed the path along the creek. We watched the different fish swim about in the cool water. We must have seen twenty trouts! On our return to the cabin, we heard the morning call of the quail, and we knew it was time for breakfast.

WRITE ON!

If you spent a week in the woods, what would you expect to see? On a separate sheet of paper, write a paragraph telling about a week spent in the woods. Use irregular plural nouns in your sentences, and underline them.

Name _____   Date _____

Collective Nouns

A **collective noun** refers to a group of people, animals, things, or ideas.

- A collective noun takes a singular verb when talking about the group as a whole.
  Example: The *team* is ready to warm up.

- A collective noun takes a plural verb when talking about different parts of the group.
  Example: Some of the *team* have done jumping jacks while others have done push-ups.

PRACTICE

Complete each sentence with the correct verb form.

1. A swarm of locusts _____ heading our way!

2. Some of the locusts _____ gigantic!

3. The members of the jury _____ casting votes.

4. The jury _____ deliberating behind closed doors.

5. The crowd _____ angry about having to wait hours for tickets.

6. Some people in the crowd _____ leaving the ticket line.

7. The class _____ waiting patiently for the teacher.

8. All of the students _____ beginning to get restless.

9. The crew _____ flown into space before.

10. The members of the crew _____ trained to do different tasks.

Think of four other collective nouns. (*Hint:* Many collective nouns name groups of animals.)

1. _____   3. _____

2. _____   4. _____

Write a sentence for each collective noun.

1. _____

2. _____

3. _____

4. _____

WRITE ON!

A school refers to a group of fish. On a separate sheet of paper, write a paragraph about fish. Check to make sure that each sentence has subject-verb agreement.

Name _____   Date _____

Helping Verbs

Helping verbs are also known as auxiliary verbs. Helping verbs do not have any meaning by themselves in a sentence. Helping verbs need to be combined with a main verb or adjective to create meaning.

Example: The dog *is* barking.

Common Helping Verbs

am	being	does	had	must	were
are	can	did	is	shall	will
be	could	has	may	should	would
been	do	have	might	was	

PRACTICE

Choose five helping verbs, and use one of them in each sentence.

Example: Kay must finish her homework before she watches television.

1. _____

2. _____

3. _____

4. _____

5. _____

Underline the helping verbs used in the paragraph. Then, write the helping verbs on the lines.

Yesterday, my dog, Dagney, was acting strangely. She had been gathering old towels and blankets and dragging them to a corner. Dagney then made a bed out of the towels and blankets. Finally, Dagney laid down in the pile of blankets. When I checked on Dagney later, you wouldn't believe what I saw. Dagney had had three puppies! Dagney was a mom!

_____ , _____ , _____ , _____

_____ , _____ , _____

WRITE ON!

Have you ever had a pet do something unusual or strange? Was there a reason for the pet's odd behavior? On a separate sheet of paper, tell about the event. Use helping verbs in the paragraph, and underline them.

Name _____   Date _____

Helping Verbs

Helping verbs are also known as auxiliary verbs. Helping verbs do not have any meaning by themselves in a sentence. Helping verbs need to be combined with a main verb or adjective to create meaning.

Example: Adam *can* eat six hot dogs in one sitting.

PRACTICE

Underline the helping verbs used in the paragraph.

Mr. Mitchell is always running behind schedule. He says that it is because he has too many things

to do. One day, he said that he might be late because his cat was stuck in a tree, and he could not

wake his dog up! His wife, Mrs. Mitchell, has even tried setting the clocks ahead by ten minutes.

She did this in hopes that it would help her husband get to his appointments on time. It worked for

a while, until the power went out, and Mr. Mitchell had to reset all of the clocks!

What else could Mr. Mitchell do to be on time for his appointments? Write your suggestions below.

1. _____

2. _____

3. _____

Use the following helping verbs in sentences.

| am | do | have | may | should | were |

1. _____

2. _____

3. _____

4. _____

5. _____

6. _____

WRITE ON!

Have you ever been late? What happened? Why were you late? Write about the day on a separate sheet of paper. Use helping verbs in your sentences, and underline them.

Name _____ Date _____

Regular and Irregular Verbs

A **regular verb** changes tense in a predictable way. For example, to change a verb from the present tense to the past tense, add *–ed* to the end of the verb.

Example: I *talk* on the phone. (*present tense*)

I *talked* on the phone. (*past tense*)

Write eight regular verbs in their present and past tense forms.

Present Tense	Past Tense
Example: wash	washed
1.	
2.	
3.	
4.	
5.	
6.	
7.	
8.	

Draw a line through the mistakes in the paragraph. Write the correct form of the verb above the line.

Saturday is laundry day at my house. We gather up all of the dirty clothes and sort the clothes into

piles by color—lights and darks, and by fabric—towels and sheets. Then, the washing starts. Once

a load of clothes is washes in the washer, the load is moving to the dryer. If the weather is nice,

sometimes the clothes are hung up on the clothesline to dry outside in the sun. Once the clothes

are dry, they are folden and placed into bins. Each family member has his or her own clothing bin.

Then, the laundry is done for the week!

On a separate sheet of paper, write about a weekend chore that your family does. Use regular present tense and past tense verbs in the paragraph, and underline them.

Name _____ Date _____

Regular and Irregular Verbs

An **irregular verb** does not change tense in a predictable way. You cannot add *–ed* to the end of an irregular verb to change its tense from present to past. Instead, the verb changes form.

>   Example: He *chooses* Max to be on his team. (*present tense*)
>   He *chose* Max to be on his team. (*past tense*)

Write the past tense of the following irregular verbs.

Present Tense	Past Tense	Present Tense	Past Tense
Example: bring	brought	Example: tell	told
1. drink		11. write	
2. keep		12. win	
3. hang		13. sleep	
4. give		14. sit	
5. make		15. think	
6. pay		16. draw	
7. run		17. see	
8. say		18. feed	
9. sting		19. leave	
10. wear		20. lie	

Draw a line through the mistakes in the paragraph. Write the correct form of the verb above the line.

   Shawn run all the way home. He was excited to tell his family the good news. He thinked his

parents would be excited for him, but he knowed his sister would think he maked it all up. He

would show them his history test, and they would see for themselves that he had paid attention in

class. They would say things like, "We are so proud of you," and "You outdoed yourself!" Shawn

feeled like he had winned the lottery!

Think of a time you did something that was a pleasant surprise for your family. What did you do? How did your family react? On a separate sheet of paper, write a paragraph that answers these questions. Use irregular verbs in the paragraph, and underline them.

Name _____ Date _____

Regular and Irregular Verbs

A **regular verb** changes tense in a predictable way. For example, to change a verb from the present tense to the past tense, add *–ed* to the end of the verb. To show the future tense, add *will* before the verb.

Example: Crews *paint* the houses. (*present tense*)

Crews *painted* the houses. (*past tense*)

Crews *will paint* the houses. (*future tense*)

PRACTICE

Answer the questions.

1. Which tense shows an action that will happen sometime in the future? _____

2. Which tense shows an action that is a fact, habit, truth, or usual activity? _____

3. Which tense shows an action that has already happened? _____

Read the paragraphs. Identify the tense.

Paragraph #1

During summer vacation, I will work at the local animal shelter. I will help take care of animals, clean cages, and help people find a new pet for their families.

Tense: _____

Paragraph #2

I have to be the luckiest person in the world! Yesterday, I found a four-leaf clover. Then, I won a free soda at the local hamburger place. Finally, I reached in my pocket and discovered a ten-dollar bill. It was my lucky day!

Tense: _____

Paragraph #3

Matt loves to play the guitar. During the weekend, he likes to look at his music book and practice playing. He is a wonderful guitar player.

Tense: _____

WRITE ON!

Using one of the tenses, write a paragraph on a topic of your choice on a separate sheet of paper. Check to make sure that the same tense was used throughout the paragraph. Exchange papers with a classmate. Ask the classmate to identify the tense used in the paragraph.

Name _____   Date _____

Regular and Irregular Verbs

An **irregular verb** does not change tense in a predictable way. Instead, the verb changes form.

Verb Tenses	Regular Verb	Irregular Verb
Present Tense	I walk to school.	I am early.
Past Tense	I walked to school.	I was early.
Future Tense	I will walk to school.	I will be early.

PRACTICE

Complete the chart to show the present tense, past tense, and future tense for each irregular verb.

Verb	Present Tense	Past Tense	Future Tense
Example: become	become	became	become
1. bring		brought	
2. grow			
3. come	come		
4. freeze			freeze
5. do			do
6. leave		left	
7. go			
8. keep			
9. arise			
10. buy	buy		
11. fly			
12. know			
13. pay			
14. break			
15. teach		taught	
16. hit			
17. ride			
18. take			

WRITE ON!

On a separate sheet of paper, use four of the irregular verbs in a paragraph. Underline the irregular verbs.

Name _____   Date _____

Regular and Irregular Verbs

Other verb tenses are present perfect, past perfect, and future perfect.

Present Perfect Tense:

- When used with *for* or *since*, it describes an action that began in the past and continues into the present.

    Example: I *have been* at school since seven o'clock.

- It describes an action that happened (or never happened) before now at an unspecified time in the past.

    Example: I *have finished* my homework assignment.

- It describes the repetition of an action before now.

    Example: We *have had* six tests so far this semester.

Past Perfect Tense: an action was completed before another action in the past.

    Example: The teacher *had* already *talked* about the research project before Daniel entered the classroom.

Future Perfect Tense: an action will be completed before another action in the future.

    Example: I *will have completed* my homework before I go to the movies tonight.

PRACTICE

Identify the underlined tense in each sentence.

    Example: I <u>have watered</u> the yard every day this week.   <u>present perfect tense</u>

1. Simon <u>will have finished</u> football practice by the time you get off of work.   _____

2. The car <u>had stopped</u> before it was rear-ended.   _____

3. The frog <u>had jumped</u> from the log before Otto noticed it was gone.   _____

4. Fred and I <u>have repaired</u> many different kinds of engines.   _____

5. The telephone repairperson <u>will have fixed</u> the line before dinner is done.   _____

6. Jen <u>has wrestled</u> for many years.   _____

Write one sentence to illustrate each verb tense.

Present Perfect Tense: _____

Past Perfect Tense: _____

Future Perfect Tense: _____

WRITE ON!

On a separate sheet of paper, write a paragraph on a topic of your choice. Use the perfect tenses in the paragraph, and underline them.

Name _____   Date _____

Adjectives

- An **adjective** describes or modifies a noun.

    Example: The *dirty* window needs to be cleaned.

- An **adjective** may follow a form of the verb *be*.

    Examples: I am *happy*.

    He is *late*.

    They are *smart*.

    She was *sick*.

    We were *hungry*.

- An **adjective** may follow a verb that describes a sense: feel, taste, smell, sound, look.

    Examples: The sneakers smell *terrible*.

    The cake tastes *delicious*.

PRACTICE

Write an adjective on each line.

    Example: <u>orange</u> chicken

1. _____ shirt   4. _____ book

2. _____ computer   5. _____ hair

3. _____ gorilla   6. _____ sneakers

Write four adjectives that describe a bird.

_____ , _____ , _____ , _____

Use the adjectives in a short paragraph about a bird.

_____

_____

_____

_____

WRITE ON!

On a separate sheet of paper, write five adjectives that describe your appearance, personality, or attitude. Use the five adjectives in a paragraph.

Name _____   Date _____

Adjectives

- An **adjective** describes or modifies a noun.

    Example: The *filthy* car needs to be cleaned.

- An **adjective** may follow a form of the verb *be*.

    Examples: I am *tired*.

    They are *excited*.

    He is *nervous*.

    She was *surprised*.

    We were *upset*.

- An **adjective** may follow a verb that describes a sense: feel, taste, smell, sound, look.

    Examples: The socks feel *soft*.

    That man looks *frightened*.

PRACTICE

Complete each sentence with an adjective.

1. Greg had been _____ .

2. The dog is _____ .

3. The refrigerator is _____ .

4. Sheldon was _____ .

5. The meal was _____ .

6. The giraffe's sneeze sounded _____ .

7. The sandpaper felt _____ .

8. The players appeared _____ .

9. The painting looked _____ .

10. The snail tasted _____ .

11. The monster looks _____ .

12. I feel _____ .

WRITE ON!

On a separate sheet of paper, write four sentences. Exchange papers with a classmate. Ask the classmate to add an adjective to each sentence.

Name _____   Date _____

Adjectives

An **adjective** describes or modifies a noun. An adjective answers one of the following three questions:

- **What kind is it?**

    Example: Gage ate the smelly, rotten egg.

    What kind of egg? the *smelly, rotten* egg

- **How many are there?**

    Example: The seven pizzas were for the winning class.

    How many pizzas? *seven* pizzas

- **Which one is it?**

    Example: The green apple is for the teacher.

    Which apple? the *green* apple

Sometimes two or more adjectives are used to describe a noun.

- Use a comma if they are coordinate adjectives. Coordinate adjectives can be switched or have the word *and* put in between them and the sentence still makes sense.

    Example: The *big*, *juicy* watermelon is ready to be picked.

    The *big* and *juicy* watermelon is ready to be picked.

- Non-coordinate adjectives do not need commas. Sentences with non-coordinate adjectives do not make sense if their order is changed or when the word *and* is put in between them.

    Example: Lindsey wore a *bright pink* vest to school.

    Lindsey wore a *pink bright* vest to school. (This sentence does not make sense.)

Add commas to the sentences with coordinate adjectives.

    Example: Sienna has a new, flashy sports car.

1. The thin decomposing lighthouse has guided ships and sailors for many years.

2. The short redheaded child wants a balloon.

3. The old leather couch was bought for the new house.

4. My grandma wore a long loud muumuu to the party.

5. The coldhearted hardheaded miser refused to give a penny to the orphan.

6. The fire department raced to rescue the fat fluffy feline stuck in a tree.

On a separate sheet of paper, write four sentences with at least two adjectives in each sentence. Circle the sentences that contain coordinate adjectives.

Name _____ Date _____

Comparative Adjectives

A **comparative adjective** compares two people, places, things, or ideas.

- For most one-syllable adjectives, add an –er to the end of the adjective. (If the adjective ends in –y, drop the –y and add –ier.)

  Example: (dry) The air is *drier* today than it was yesterday.

- For most two-syllable adjectives, add *more* or *less* before the adjective. For some two-syllable words, add –er or –ier to the end of the adjective.

  Examples: (handsome) My dog is *more handsome* than your dog.

  (happy) Rosie is *happier* than Sophie.

- For adjectives with three or more syllables, use *more* or *less* before the adjective.

  Example: (intelligent) Fred is *less intelligent* than Barney.

Write the correct comparative adjective on the line.

Example: (long) Her hair is <u>longer</u> than Molly's.

1. (vibrant) Chaz's tie is _____ than Jake's tie.

2. (confused) Alex is _____ by the teacher's directions than Alicia.

3. (clever) Ryan is _____ than Steve.

4. (strong) The weightlifter is _____ than the ballerina.

5. (crazy) That stunt was _____ than last year's!

6. (comfortable) This chair is _____ than the bean bag.

7. (pretty) The doll is _____ than the stuffed animal.

8. (flashy) Liberace was a _____ performer than Don Ho.

9. (popular) The new singer is _____ than Diva Devine.

10. (alike) The identical twins look _____ than the fraternal twins.

11. (healthy) Fruits and vegetables are _____ than cake and candy.

12. (trivial) This argument is _____ than the last one!

On a separate sheet of paper, write a paragraph comparing two different people, places, things, or ideas. Underline the comparative adjective used in each sentence.

Name _____   Date _____

Superlative Adjectives

A **superlative adjective** compares three or more people, places, things, or ideas.

- For one-syllable adjectives, add *–est* to the end of the adjective. If the adjective ends in *–y*, drop the *–y* and add *–iest*.

    Example: (tall) Amanda is the *tallest* girl in the class.

- For some two-syllable adjectives, add *–est* to the end of it. For most two-syllable words, use *most* or *least* before the adjective.

    Examples: (shiny) This is the *shiniest* penny!

    (gorgeous) George was voted the *most gorgeous* boy in the school.

- For three-syllable adjectives, use *most* or *least* before the adjective.

    Example: (beautiful) Isabella is the *most beautiful* baby in the world.

Complete each sentence with the correct superlative adjective.

1. (crazy) This was the _____ idea that Gilligan has ever had.

2. (lucky) Hannah is the _____ person!

3. (colorful) That painting is the _____ one in the museum.

4. (interesting) Amanda's solution is the _____ .

5. (gracious) Nellie is the _____ hostess.

6. (efficient) The new hybrid car is the _____ one on the market.

7. (trouble) Who got into the _____ today?

8. (loud) The drum player is the _____ one in the band.

9. (urgent) This was the _____ message the superhero had ever received.

10. (delicious) The apple pie was the _____ one I had ever tasted.

11. (bright) The sun is the _____ at midday.

12. (fresh) The farmer's market has the _____ produce.

On a separate sheet of paper, use superlative adjectives to describe the best day or the worst day of your life. Share your paragraph with a classmate.

Name _____ Date _____

Comparative and Superlative Adjectives

A **comparative adjective** compares two people, places, things, or ideas. A **superlative adjective** compares three or more people, places, things, or ideas. Some two-syllable words are unique. They can be made comparative or superlative in two different ways.

- To make them comparative, add *–er* or use the word *more* in front of the adjective.
- To make them superlative, add *–est* or use the word *most* in front of the adjective.

  Example: Sal is a friendly person.

  Tim is a *friendlier* person than Sal.   *or*   Tim is a *more friendly* person than Sal.

  Shanice is the *friendliest* of all.   *or*   Shanice is the *most friendly* of all.

Comparative and Superlative Adjectives That Can Be Written Two Ways

common	gentle	pleasant	simple
friendly	narrow	quiet	useless

PRACTICE

Use each adjective as a comparative or superlative adjective in a sentence.

1. (simple) _____

2. (gentle) _____

3. (narrow) _____

4. (friendly) _____

5. (pleasant) _____

Draw a line through the mistakes. Write the correct form of the adjective above the line.

Over a hundred years ago, the most cleverest people made this bridge. The bridge is of the most simpler design, just wood and rope. The bridge spans the most narrowest part of the Giganto River. Most of the time, the moving water makes the more quietest of sounds. During heavy rain, the moving water becomes less pleasanter. Instead, the water becomes a raging river. The bridge and river are an amazing sight to see.

WRITE ON!

On a separate sheet of paper, write about a clever invention you have seen or used, or something you would like to see invented. Use comparative and superlative adjectives in the paragraph, and underline them.

Name _____ Date _____

Irregular Comparative and Superlative Adjectives

Some **adjectives** change form when comparing items.

    Example: Carmen is *good* at math.

        Max is *better* at math than Carmen.

        Luisa is the *best* of all.

Complete the chart.

Adjective	Comparative (two items)	Superlative (three or more items)
good		best
bad		worst
far	farther	
little	less	
many		most

Underline the adjective in the first sentence. Complete each set of sentences with the correct form of the comparative and superlative adjectives.

1. Jerome has little money saved for the field trip.

    Nadine has _____ money saved for the field trip than Jerome.

    Georgette has the _____ amount of money saved of all.

2. Danny has many comic books in his collection.

    Fran has _____ in her collection than Danny.

    Lara has the _____ comic books of all.

3. Ophelia feels bad about losing the game.

    Robin feels _____ than Ophelia about losing the game.

    Kathy feels the _____ of all.

4. This is a good movie.

    The book is _____ than the movie.

    The play is the _____ of all.

On a separate sheet of paper, write a paragraph comparing three items. Use comparative and superlative adjectives in the paragraph, and underline them.

Name _____   Date _____

Adjectives and Adverbs—Bad or Badly?

Bad or badly? Which one should be used?

- When describing one's health or emotions, use *bad*. *Bad* is an adjective. *Bad* means not good or correct. *Bad* describes the noun. Remember to use *bad* if it follows a sense verb.

    Example: Tim feels bad.

    Bad means that Tim does not feel well. Tim is sick.

- When describing how one performs, use *badly*. *Badly* is an adverb. *Badly* describes the verb. When in doubt, try substituting the word *poorly* for *badly*. If *poorly* makes sense in the sentence, then the word to use is *badly*.

    Example: John played the violin badly.

    Badly means that John does not play the violin well.

PRACTICE

Which word, *bad* or *badly*, should be used? Read each set of sentences. Write *bad* or *badly* on the line.

1. Magda woke up with a fever, and now her stomach is upset. Magda feels _____ .

2. Paul is horrible at telling jokes. He always messes up the punch line. Paul tells jokes _____ .

3. Miranda lost her kitty. She looked everywhere for it. Miranda feels _____ .

4. Gray lost all sensation in his fingers. He cannot hold his pencil. Gray feels _____ .

5. Duncan ate everything on his plate, and now his stomach hurts. Duncan feels _____ .

6. Amy missed her lunch date and is sad about it. Amy feels _____ .

7. The movie was terrible. It was the worst movie ever made. The movie was _____ .

8. It took Jerry three days to return his mother's phone call. Jerry responded _____ .

9. The paint was old. It did not cover the wall correctly. The paint was _____ .

10. Terri micromanages everybody. She is not a good manager. She manages _____ .

WRITE ON!

On a separate sheet of paper, write four sentences. In two of the sentences, use the word *bad*. In the other two sentences, use the word *badly*. Exchange papers with a classmate. Ask the classmate to make sure the words were used correctly.

Name _____   Date _____

Adjectives and Adverbs—Good or Well?

Good or well? Which one should be used?

- *Good* is an adjective. *Good* follows forms of the verb *be* as well as sense verbs.

  Examples: I feel good.

  The food tastes good.

- *Well* can be an adjective, if it is describing a person's health.

  Example: I feel well.

- *Well* is an adverb when it is not describing a person's health.

  Example: I did well on the test.

Complete each sentence with *good* or *well*.

1. I feel _____ about how the team played.

2. The team played the game _____ .

3. Nancy is not feeling _____ today.

4. Luna is a _____ pet.

5. We scored _____ while playing darts.

6. Marvin did a _____ deed.

7. Marlon always does _____ on the weekly spelling test.

8. Amanda is _____ at playing many sports.

9. Jamie's hearing is _____ .

10. The wires are not connected _____ , and that's why the reception is bad.

11. If you want to stay _____ , eat plenty of fruits and vegetables.

12. The singers sound _____ from the back row of the auditorium.

13. The desserts all smell _____ .

14. Luigi plays the piano _____ .

Luna

On a separate sheet of paper, tell about something you are good at. Underline the words *good* and *well*.
Check to make sure you used each word correctly in its sentence.

Name _____   Date _____

Adjectives and Adverbs—Real or Really?

Real or really? Which one should be used?

- *Real* is an adjective.

   Example: I have a real dog.

- *Really* is an adverb. When in doubt, try substituting *very* for *really*. If *very* makes sense in the sentence, then *really* is the word to use.

   Example: This food tastes really (very) good.

PRACTICE

Complete the story using *real* and *really*.

Sally and Charlotte were _____ good friends. They liked to do arts and crafts

together. They usually met at Sally's house because her craft room was _____

neat and tidy. Charlotte kept her craft supplies in the _____ tall closet.

Charlotte carefully opened her box and picked out some _____ tiny beads.

Charlotte was _____ good at beading. She made all kinds of necklaces and

bracelets for people. People said that she had a _____ talent for beading. Sally

kept her supplies in the tall closet, too. Sally had _____ flowers drying in a

box and plastic flowers in a different box. Sally had fun at flower arranging. She could even make

plastic flowers look _____ . People were amazed at her skills.

Write two sentences using the word *real*.

   1. _____

   2. _____

Write two sentences using the word *really*.

   1. _____

   2. _____

WRITE ON!

What kinds of crafts do you like to do? What kinds of crafts would you like to learn how to do? On a separate sheet of paper, write a paragraph on this topic. Use the words *real* and *really* in the paragraph, and underline them. Check to make sure each word was used correctly in its sentence.

Name _____ Date _____

Adverbs

An **adverb** describes a verb, an adjective, or another adverb. An adverb answers one of the following questions:

- **How?**   The pencil snapped loudly in half.
  How did the pencil snap? loudly
- **When?**   My pencil snapped today.
  When did the pencil snap? today
- **Where?**   The pencil snapped inside.
  Where did the pencil snap? inside
- **Why?**   The pencil snapped because Anthony pressed too hard.
  Why did the pencil snap? because Anthony pressed too hard
- **In what order?** The pencil snapped first.
  In what order did the pencil snap? first

Common Adverbs

almost	far	much	once	somewhat	usually
always	fast	never	only	then	very
daily	hard	next	rarely	there	well
early	here	not	seldom	today	yesterday
even	less	now	so	tomorrow	
everywhere	more	often	sometimes	twice	

PRACTICE

Use six of the adverbs, and write each one in a sentence. Write what question each adverb answers.

      Example: I went quickly to the store.   <u>How</u>

1. _____ _____
2. _____ _____
3. _____ _____
4. _____ _____
5. _____ _____
6. _____ _____

On a separate sheet of paper, tell about something that does not happen very often. Use at least three adverbs in the paragraph. Underline the adverbs.

Name _____   Date _____

Adverbs

An **adverb** describes a verb, an adjective, or another adverb. Many adverbs end in –*ly*.

    Example: Sara walked *quickly* down the street.

PRACTICE

Underline the adverb(s) in each sentence.

    Example: The recess bell rang <u>loudly</u>.

1. Alexander jumped lightly over the fence.

2. It wanted to play nicely with all of the children.

3. The children ran quickly away from Alexander.

4. They were terribly afraid of being scratched.

5. Alexander sat patiently on the grass and played with a bug.

6. The children slowly walked towards Alexander.

7. First, one child reached out to pat Alexander.

8. Alexander gently licked her hand.

9. Jack went next.

10. The child giggled delightfully at the feel of Alexander's tongue.

11. Soon, all of the children were wrestling playfully with Alexander.

12. When the bell rang, Alexander jumped gracefully back over the fence.

13. The children sincerely promised to play with him again.

14. The children noisily lined up.

Write an adverb to describe each event.

1. How did the toucan sing?   _____

2. How did the bear walk?   _____

3. How did the bird fly?   _____

4. How did the frog leap?   _____

WRITE ON!

Have you ever had something surprising and exciting happen to you? On a separate sheet of paper, write about it. Use adverbs in the paragraph, and underline them.

Name _____ Date _____

Adverbs

An **adverb** describes a verb, an adjective, or another adverb. Adverbs can be sorted into different categories.

- Adverbs of **manner** tell *how* it happened or was done.
- Adverbs of **place** tell *where* it happened.
- Adverbs of **frequency** tell *how often* or *how many times* it happened.
- Adverbs of **time** tell *when* it happened or *how long* it happened.
- Adverbs of **purpose** tell *why* it happened.

Sort the adverbs into the different categories.

abroad	easily	next	patiently	since
after	fast	now	quietly	so that
because	here	often	rarely	somewhere
before	in order to	outside	seldom	usually

Manner	Place	Frequency	Time	Purpose
1.	1.	1.	1.	1.
2.	2.	2.	2.	2.
3.	3.	3.	3.	3.
4.	4.	4.	4.	4.

Use an adverb from each category in a sentence. Underline the adverb in each sentence.

Example: The pig <u>rarely</u> squealed.

1. _____
2. _____
3. _____
4. _____
5. _____

On a separate sheet of paper, explain the difference between an adjective and an adverb. Share your explanation with a classmate.

Name _____ Date _____

DAILY
Warm-Up 43

Comparative and Superlative Adverbs

An **adverb** describes a verb, an adjective, or another adverb. A **comparative adverb** compares how two things were done. To make a comparative adverb, add *–er* to the end of the adverb. If the adverb ends in *–ly*, add the word *more* or *less* before the adverb.

Examples: Bill ran *faster* than Tom.

Bill ran *more quickly* than Tom.

A **superlative adverb** compares how three or more things were done. To make a superlative adverb, add *–est* to the end of the adverb. If the adverb ends in *–ly*, add the word *most* or *least* before the adverb.

Examples: Sue ran the *fastest* of all.

Sue ran *most quickly* of all.

PRACTICE

Write four adverbs.

Examples: smoothly, fast, foolishly, soon

_____ , _____ , _____ , _____

Use each adverb in a comparative sentence.

Example: Peter arrived sooner than Roger.

1. _____

2. _____

3. _____

4. _____

Use each adverb in a superlative sentence.

Example: Ray arrived the soonest of all.

1. _____

2. _____

3. _____

4. _____

WRITE ON!

What is the craziest thing you have ever done? On a separate sheet of paper, write about the experience. Use at least one comparative adverb and one superlative adverb in the paragraph.

Name _____ Date _____

Adverbial Phrases

An **adverb** describes a verb, an adjective, or another adverb. An adverb can be a single word, such as *quickly*, or it can be a phrase, such as *with his fingers*. Like single adverbs, **adverbial phrases** still answer *how it was done, when it was done, where it was done*, and *why it was done*.

    Examples: She ran *next door*.

              She yelled *because her toe hurt*.

Complete each sentence with an adverb or an adverbial phrase.

    Example: Gracie slept <u>because she was exhausted</u>.
                              (why?)

  1. Bill was late for work _____ .
                                       (why?)

  2. Tiffany completes her homework _____ .
                                       (how?)

  3. The judge made a ruling _____ .
                                       (how?)

  4. The celebration was held _____ .
                                       (when?)

  5. The skyscraper was built _____ .
                                       (why?)

  6. The ship hit the pier _____ .
                                       (how?)

  7. I drank a glass of water _____ .
                                       (when?)

  8. The farmer tended the animals_____ .
                                       (where?

  9. The mountain climber scaled the mountain_____ .
                                       (why?)

10. The Stevensons have lived in the home _____ .
                                       (where?)

On a separate sheet of paper, write about the chores a farmer would have to do. Use at least three adverbial phrases in the paragraph. Exchange papers with a classmate. Ask the classmate to underline the adverbial phrases and write the question each phrase answers.

Name _____ Date _____

Prepositions

A **preposition** indicates the location of an item.

> Examples: The encyclopedia is *on* the stand.
>
> The child is hiding *behind* the sofa.

PRACTICE

Circle the prepositions or prepositional phrases that tell about a location.

across	at	in front of	next to	on top of	over
among	before	near	on the back of	out of	under

Complete each sentence with one of the prepositions or prepositional phrases above.

> Example: The green alien is hiding <u>among</u> the trees.

1. The dog loves to sleep _____ the coffee table.

2. Put the printer _____ the computer.

3. Jeff is _____ the rest of the class.

4. The jack-in-the-box jumped _____ its box.

5. Mrs. Carlson's class is _____ Mr. Smith's class.

6. What is _____ your shirt?

7. I left my bike _____ the fire hydrant.

8. The grandparents are waiting _____ the house.

9. My present for you is _____ the rest of the gifts.

10. The arcade is _____ the street.

Underline the prepositions or prepositional phrases that tell about a location of an item in the paragraph.

Each day after school, Samantha throws her backpack on her bed. She pulls her headphones out from under her pillow and listens to music on her radio. When she is done, she puts the headphones and radio on top of her dresser. Samantha opens her backpack and takes out her binder. In the front of the binder is her agenda. Samantha opens the agenda to see what assignments she needs to do. She finds paper inside her desk drawer and gets to work.

WRITE ON!

On a separate sheet of paper, tell about your after-school routine. Use prepositions in the paragraph, and underline them.

Prepositions

A **preposition** indicates the location of an item.

> Examples: Put the drink *on* the counter.
>
> The palm tree is growing *in between* the two pine trees.

Common Prepositions or Prepositional Phrases That Indicate Location

above	below	by	in front of	on	past
across	beneath	down	inside	on top of	to
against	beside	from	near	out	toward
among	between	in	next to	outside	under
behind	beyond	in back of	off	over	up

PRACTICE

Answer each question with a complete sentence. Circle the preposition or prepositional phrase that indicates location in the answer.

Question	Answer
Example: Has anyone seen my baseball glove?	It's (over by) the television set.
1. Where did I put the final exams?	_____
2. Where is the nearest library?	_____
3. Which way do I go on the highway?	_____
4. Have you seen the star of the show?	_____
5. Where is the principal's office?	_____
6. Where did the dog bury its bone?	_____
7. What did the mechanic do to the car?	_____
8. Which plant is the tea rose?	_____
9. Which shop sells the best chocolates?	_____
10. Where do all of the oil pastels go?	_____

WRITE ON!

Look at a part of the classroom. On a separate sheet of paper, describe the location of the items in that area. Use prepositions in each sentence, and underline them.

Name _____ Date _____

Prepositions

A **preposition** indicates the location of an item.

  Example: The bird is sitting *in* its nest.

A **preposition** can also indicate the location in time.

  Example: *In* an hour, the bird will leave.

Prepositions That Indicate the Location in Time

at	between	for	on	till	upon
after	by	from	past	to	up to
before	during	in	since	until	within

Circle the sentences that use prepositions to indicate the location in time.

1. Alice put her books on the coffee table.

2. After watching the news, Dad went to sleep.

3. Between innings, the crowd stood up and stretched.

4. Inga hasn't missed a day of school since kindergarten.

5. The post office is past the dry cleaners.

6. Within the hour, we will have a fire drill.

7. The lion cub climbed into the tree.

8. Until now, David had never had a cavity.

9. The woman is next in line.

10. From now on, nobody should be late to practice.

11. During a moment of silence, Thomas sneezed loudly.

12. The plane will land on the runway.

Do you do something with a family member on a regular basis, such as going out to breakfast, having a family game night, or eating dinner together? On a separate sheet of paper, write about it. Use prepositions that indicate location in time, and underline them.

Name _____ Date _____

Prepositions

A **preposition** indicates the location of an item.

> Example: The bus is parked *by* the curb.

A **preposition** can also indicate the location in time.

> Example: *Before* leaving the house, I always check my backpack.

Underline the preposition that indicates location in time.

> Example: <u>Around</u> lunchtime, Berta's stomach grumbled with hunger.

1. We always get ice cream after soccer practice.

2. Before jumping into the water, make sure it is the deep end.

3. At midnight, everyone should be sound asleep.

4. Throughout the entire movie, the couple would not stop talking.

5. Between rounds, let's stop off at the club house for a soda.

6. The cuckoo clock chirps upon each hour.

7. Over dinner, we discussed the day's events.

8. The doctor will see you within the hour.

9. Next time, we should pre-order tickets to the concert.

10. The principal asked the audience not to leave until the play was over.

11. Until now, Justin had always been on time for work.

12. Near closing time, a last-minute shopper came in looking for a gift.

Write two sentences that use prepositions to indicate location in time. Underline the prepositions.

1. _____

2. _____

What is your favorite thing to do after a hard day? Write your answer on a separate sheet of paper. Use prepositions that indicate location in time, and underline them.

Parts of Speech

Name _____ Date _____

Coordinating Conjunctions

A **coordinating conjunction** connects words in a sentence. There are seven coordinating conjunctions: *for, and, nor, but, or, yet, so.* When a coordinating conjunction joins two independent clauses, use a comma before the conjunction. (Remember, an independent clause is a group of related words with a subject and a verb. It can stand alone.)

Example: Bill ate the whole thing, *and* now he has a stomachache.

Each coordinating conjunction has its own meaning:

- **For:** to show an implication (If not sure, try substituting *because* or *since*. If one of these words works, then *for* is the conjunction to use.)
- **And:** to show ideas are sequential in order or that one idea is the result of another
- **Nor:** to show a negative element or expression
- **But:** to show contrast between two ideas
- **Or:** to show a choice
- **Yet:** to give additional, contrasting ideas or information
- **So:** to give additional information or to sum up information

PRACTICE

Complete each sentence with the correct coordinating conjunction. (Use each conjunction one time.)

1. Betty removed the old carpeting, _____ she installed the new flooring.

2. Harris does not like peanuts, _____ does he like shellfish.

3. We won three cakes at the cake walk, _____ we gave one to our neighbor and one to our friend.

4. We can go skiing in the mountains, _____ we can go whitewater rafting at the river.

5. Chad was on time for his appointment, _____ the dentist was running behind schedule.

6. Norman was chosen as the team mascot, _____ he looks just like a bulldog.

7. The store was going out of business, _____ the workers had not been paid.

Use each conjunction in a sentence.

1 (for) _____

2. (yet) _____

WRITE ON!

Pretend your school is picking a new mascot, a costumed person or an animal. What qualities would you want the mascot to have? What should the mascot be able to do? Answer these questions on a separate sheet of paper. Use coordinating conjunctions in your sentences, and underline them.

Name _____   Date _____

Correlative Conjunctions

Correlative conjunctions always come in pairs. Correlative conjunctions join words, phrases, or sentences that are grammatically equal.

Example: *Both* Liza *and* Matt are great chefs.

- When joining singular and plural subjects, the subject closest to the verb determines whether the verb is singular or plural.

Examples: *Either* Sigmund *or* the twins are responsible for the accident.

Either the twins *or* Sigmund is responsible for the accident.

Common Correlative Conjunctions

as, as	either, or	not only, but also
both, and	neither, nor	whether, or

PRACTICE

Write the correct pair of correlative conjunctions on the lines.

1. _____ you go _____ I go, but we both can't share this room!

2. _____ Jason _____ Max got in trouble for throwing rocks at the windows.

3. _____ long _____ you are here, let's start painting the kitchen.

4. _____ Ogden _____ Perry were explorers.

5. _____ Primo _____ Sabrina are beautiful horses.

6. _____ this one is the correct answer, _____ it is that one.

7. Seth can _____ stay home _____ go to school; the decision is his to make.

8. At the beach, _____ cats _____ dogs are allowed to go off-leash.

9. _____ parents _____ teachers can chaperone the students.

10. _____ my parents _____ my doctor will let me do extreme wrestling.

11. _____ sugar is good for you _____ bad for you is open to debate.

12. _____ you are ready _____ not, the show must go on!

WRITE ON!

On a separate sheet of paper, write about some choices you have had to make. Use correlative conjunctions in the paragraph, and underline them.

Subordinating Conjunctions

A **subordinating conjunction** comes at the beginning of a dependent clause. (Remember, a dependent clause is a group of related words with a subject and a verb. It cannot stand alone.) The subordinating conjunction tells the relationship between the dependent clause and the independent clause.

Example: *After* they had thought about it a lot, the parents made a decision.

Common Subordinating Conjunctions

after	as though	if	since	unless	whereas
although	because	if only	so that	until	wherever
as	before	now that	than	when	while
as if	even if	once	that	whenever	
as long as	even though	rather than	though	where	

PRACTICE

Complete each sentence with a subordinating conjunction.

Example: Mom made dinner <u>even though</u> she wanted to go out to a restaurant.

1. Now you tell me _____ I already did all of this work!

2. _____ it's safe, you may cross the busy street.

3. Connie ran _____ she was being chased by a pack of wild dogs.

4. _____ the teams are ready, the game can begin.

5. _____ the manager quit, the workers had never been on strike.

6. The ambulance driver will not turn on the siren _____ it is an emergency.

7. _____ the shortage is over, please conserve the water.

8. _____ the president is visiting, the police department is out in full force.

9. _____ disaster strikes, the Red Cross is always there to provide aid and assistance.

10. Take your cell phone _____ you go.

Write two sentences with subordinating conjunctions.

1. _____

2. _____

WRITE ON!

On a separate sheet of paper, tell about a time you had to wait for someone to pick you up. What happened? Did you think they forgot about you? What changes were made so that it wouldn't happen again? Use subordinating conjunctions in the paragraph, and underline them.

Name _____   Date _____

Conjunction Confusion—Than and Then

Sometimes the words *then* and *than* can sound very much alike, but they have two completely different meanings.

- *Than* is used for comparing two choices. *Than* is a conjunction.

   Example: I would rather have chicken pox *than* have my wisdom teeth removed.

- *Then* is a time marker. It is also used to show the sequence of events. *Then* is an adverb.

   Examples: He built the fort, and *then* he made a moat.

   Back *then*, I had to walk many miles to get to school.

PRACTICE

Complete each sentence with *than* or *then*.

1. I would rather kiss a frog _____ go to the dance alone.

2. _____ what happened?

3. We worked in the yard, and _____ we went inside the house.

4. Anthony smiled when he earned the medal, and _____ he cried when the national anthem was played.

5. Barry went to the market, and _____ he went to the show.

6. The mail carrier delivered the mail, and _____ she stopped for lunch.

7. My computer crashed, and _____ the washer overflowed.

8. Misty would like this dress better _____ that pantsuit.

9. It's better to keep your animals in the backyard _____ risk having Animal Control pick them up.

10. First he stretched the canvas, and _____ he painted the portrait.

11. Open your eyes, and _____ slowly stretch your arms up to the ceiling.

12. Mr. Gibson likes it better when the store is packed with customers _____ when it's quiet and empty.

13. Which university is better _____ Lawton University?

14. Mel closed his eyes, and _____ he ate the chocolate-covered ants.

WRITE ON!

On a separate sheet of paper, explain when to use *then* and when to use *than*. Share your answer with a classmate.

Conjunction Confusion—Like, As, Such

Sometimes the words *like, as,* and *such* are used as **conjunctions**.

- *Like* is a preposition. It is used to introduce a prepositional phrase.

    Example: He eats *like* an elephant.

- *Like* can also be used to show similarities between two items.

    Example: Rubber, *like* many petroleum-based products, is damaging to the environment.

- *As* is a subordinating conjunction. It is used to introduce a dependent clause.

    Example: *As* I had mentioned earlier, today was not a good day for the stock market.

- *Such* is used to introduce a series of items.

    Example: In the city, there are many great historical homes, *such* as the Meux Home and
    Kearney Mansion.

PRACTICE

Complete each sentence with *like, as,* or *such*.

1. It looks _____ it will rain today.

2. Some foods, _____ as the tomato and pumpkin, are considered fruits by
   some people and vegetables by others.

3. Due to the cost of fuel, some airlines, _____ as Speedy Air and Zippy
   Airlines, are charging for each checked bag.

4. His problem, _____ I see it, is that he is too stubborn to accept help.

5. _____ I told you before, you cannot go to the party.

6. Last year, _____ this year, we will spend our holidays at the coast.

7. The scrawny mutt looks _____ a chinchilla.

8. Other modes of transportation, _____ as bicycles, buses, and scooters, are
   becoming popular.

Use each word as a conjunction in a sentence.

1. (like)_____

2. (as) _____

3. (such) _____

WRITE ON!

On a separate sheet of paper, write a paragraph about items that are made from petroleum products. Use
like, as, and *such* in the paragraph.

Name _____   Date _____

Interjections

An **interjection** shows strong emotion, such as anger, happiness, surprise, enjoyment, and sorrow. It is usually one word that is separated from the rest of the sentence by a comma, period, or exclamation point.

Example: *Wow*! Did you see that?

Underline the interjection in each sentence.

1. Ouch! That bee stung me on the arm.

2. Whoa! You need to slow down.

3. Aha! I found the secret gold mine.

4. Yikes! That red car almost hit the blue car in the right lane.

5. Eeek! There's a mouse in the kitchen cupboard.

6. Ugggh, not broccoli lasagna again!

7. Wait! I'm going as fast as I can go.

8. Phew! I'm glad that is over.

9. Sweet! Did you see her steal the ball back?

10. Ooops! I spilled paint all over the floor.

11. Well, the caterpillar crawled under the leaf.

12. Yes, I can help you at the snack bar.

13. Uh oh, somebody's in trouble now.

14. Oh, I've seen that movie before.

15. No, I don't want to eat there again.

16. Help! I've fallen and can't get up!

17. Ahhhhhh, what a sweet baby.

18. Wow! I love the paint job on your motorcycle.

Name four other words that you use as interjections.

1. _____   3. _____

2. _____   4. _____

On a separate sheet of paper, write five sentences using interjections.

Name _____ Date _____

Types of Sentences

There are four types of sentences: declarative, interrogative (question), imperative (command or request), and exclamatory.

- A **declarative sentence** makes a statement. It begins with a capital letter and ends with a period.

    Example: I like to ride my pink bicycle.

- An **interrogative sentence** asks a question. An interrogative sentence begins with a capital letter and ends with a question mark.

    Example: Do you like to ride your pink bicycle?

- An **imperative sentence** is a command or a request. In an imperative sentence, the subject (*you*) is implied. An imperative sentence begins with a capital letter and ends with a period.

    Example: Ride your bike.

- An **exclamatory sentence** shows strong emotion. An exclamatory sentence begins with a capital letter and ends with an exclamation point.

    Example: I love to ride my bike!

PRACTICE

Write the type of sentence on each line.

1. We went to Pete's Pizza Parlor for lunch.   _____

2. Eat your lunch.   _____

3. The pizza was fantastic!   _____

4. What kind of pizza do you like?   _____

Read the paragraph. Add the correct ending punctuation to each sentence.

The Golden Gate Bridge is in San Francisco, California   Do you know when the bridge was finished   It was finished in 1937   It took four years to build, and they actually finished it under budget   At the time, it was the longest suspension bridge in the world   The bridge is painted a color called international orange   The architect of the bridge thought that this color was more appropriate than gray or black

WRITE ON!

On a separate sheet of paper, write a paragraph on a topic of your choice. Incorporate all four sentence types into the paragraph.

Simple Sentences

There are four other kinds of sentences: simple, compound, complex, and compound-complex.

A **simple sentence** is one independent clause. It does not contain transitional words or dependent clauses.

Example: Wendy has a red wagon.

Look at each pair of sentences. Circle the simple sentence.

1. The train chugged slowly down the track, and then it pulled to a stop at the station.

   The train stopped.

2. The door shut.

   Andre slammed the door shut before running out to play.

3. The doctor did rounds.

   While at the hospital, the doctor did her morning rounds.

4. Mrs. Brown is a kind person.

   Without a doubt, Mrs. Brown is a nice person.

5. The lights flickered.

   The lights flickered in the moonlight, and then they went completely out.

Read the paragraph. Underline the simple sentences.

The movie crew started filming. First, the actor acted like he was going to jump off of the building, but then the stunt double took over. The stunt double jumped. He landed gently onto a giant airbag. In the next scene, the actor was behind the wheel of a fancy sports car. The film crew made it look like the car was being driven at a high rate of speed, but in reality it was being pulled slowly down the street by a large truck. When the scene was over, the actor got out of the car and returned to his trailer. He wanted to rest.

Write three simple sentences.

1. _____

2. _____

3. _____

Use only simple sentences to tell about a topic of your choice. Write these on a separate sheet of paper.

Name _____   Date _____

Compound Sentences

There are four other kinds of sentences: simple, compound, complex, and compound-complex.

A **compound sentence** is made from two or more simple sentences (independent clauses) joined by a coordinating conjunction. (The coordinating conjunctions are: *for, and, nor, but, or, yet, so.*)

Examples: Ty tried to speak Spanish. His friend tried to speak Mandarin. (simple sentences)

Ty tried to speak Spanish, and his friend tried to speak Mandarin. (compound sentence)

Combine the simple sentences into one compound sentence.

1. Tracy worked on the car. She built a tree house.

   _____

2. Vic watched the latest action movie. He ate a huge tub of popcorn.

   _____

3. Bonnie and Len wanted to do something fun. They made a house out of playing cards.

   _____

4. Tina's alarm clock did not go off. She missed the bus.

   _____

5. Nick thought he was a shoe-in for the job. He botched the entire interview.

   _____

6. Kim completed her homework. Rover ate the assignments.

   _____

7. The chef prepared dinner. The baker made the dessert.

   _____

8. The singer went on tour. Her family stayed home.

   _____

Write two compound sentences. Circle the coordinating conjunction in each sentence.

1. _____

2. _____

On a separate sheet of paper, write a paragraph on a topic of your choice. Underline the compound sentences. (Remember, a compound sentence can be separated into two simple sentences.)

Name _____ Date _____

Complex Sentences

There are four other kinds of sentences: simple, compound, complex, and compound-complex.

A **complex sentence** has two parts: a simple sentence (independent clause) and a dependent clause. A subordinating conjunction is used to connect the dependent clause to the independent clause.

Examples: When I was little, I liked to ride my pink bike.

I liked to ride my pink bike when I was little.

Subordinating Conjunctions

Time	Place	Cause	Condition	Contrast
when	where	because	if	although
whenever	wherever	since	unless	even though
while		now that		despite
since		as		in spite of
before				
after				
until				
once				

PRACTICE

Add a dependent clause to change each simple sentence into a complex sentence.

Example: Uncle Jeff went sailing.

In spite of the bad weather, Uncle Jeff went sailing.

1. Beth babysits the neighborhood children.

   _____

2. Mom said that I could stay up late.

   _____

3. The bakery had two fruit pies left.

   _____

4. We made a sandcastle.

   _____

5. My family enjoys playing board games.

   _____

WRITE ON!

On a separate sheet of paper, tell about the last time you saw fireworks—either in person or on televsion. What was the occasion? Use complex sentences in the paragraph, and underline them.

Name _____   Date _____

Compound-Complex Sentences

There are four other kinds of sentences: simple, compound, complex, and compound-complex.

A **compound-complex sentence** has two parts: a compound sentence and a dependent clause. A subordinating conjunction is used to connect the dependent clause to the compound sentence.

    Example: Because of the impending storm, my family and I closed all of the shutters, and we headed down to the basement.

Underline the compound-complex sentences used in the paragraphs.

Paragraph #1

Although I studied hard, I did not pass the test, and I will have to retake the class. This really bummed me out as I had made many summer plans. I was going to visit my Aunt CeCe. Because I don't know how to swim, my aunt had signed me up for swim lessons, and she had inquired about a course in water safety.

Paragraph #2

My great-grandpa likes to tell stories about his childhood. When he was a boy, he lived on a farm outside of town. My great-grandpa took care of the different farm animals. Early in the morning, my great-grandpa would get up, and he would head out to the barn. The first job of the day was to gather eggs from the hens. Because he didn't want the hens to peck at his hand, he would be fast, but he would also be gentle. After gathering eggs, my great-grandpa then had to milk the cows. Great-grandpa always said that there was nothing better than milk fresh from the cow! When he finished his chores, it was time for breakfast, and then it was off to the bus stop to catch the bus.

Write three compound-complex sentences. Draw one line under the dependent clause. Circle the subordinating and coordinating conjunctions.

   1. _____

   2. _____

   3. _____

Pretend you have great-grandchildren. What would you tell them about your life? Write your response on a separate sheet of paper. Use compound-complex sentences in the paragraph, and underline them.

Name _____ Date _____

Sentence Review

There are four other kinds of sentences: simple, compound, complex, and compound-complex.

- A **simple sentence** is one independent clause. It does not contain transitional words or dependent clauses.
- A **compound sentence** is made from two or more simple sentences (independent clauses) joined by a coordinating conjunction.
- A **complex sentence** has two parts: a simple sentence (independent clause) and a dependent clause. A subordinating conjunction is used to connect the dependent clause to the independent clause.
- A **compound-complex sentence** has two parts: a compound sentence and a dependent clause. A subordinating conjunction is used to connect the dependent clause to the compound sentence.

PRACTICE

Identify each type of sentence.

SS = Simple Sentence	**CS** = Compound Sentence
XS = Complex Sentence	**CX** = Compound-Complex Sentence

1. Marjorie eats strawberry jam. _____
2. Although she was new at sewing, Beatrice made a beautiful dress. _____
3. We wanted to drive across the bridge, but the bridge was closed. _____
4. After the blustery wind died down, the sailors took the boats out, and they saw the stands full of racing fans. _____
5. Jessica went home. _____
6. The fence is brown. _____
7. Before instruction starts, the teacher leads the flag salute, and Gilbert takes attendance. _____
8. My dog has long fur, and it has a short tail. _____
9. Raquel cuts hair, and she paints fingernails. _____
10. Although she was on a diet, Nancy couldn't resist eating a brownie, and she couldn't resist trying the chocolate cake. _____
11. While my mom wasn't looking, I hid her present behind the chair. _____
12. After the game was over, Cecil took the bus home. _____

WRITE ON!

On a separate sheet of paper, write a paragraph using all four kinds of sentences.

Name _____   Date _____

Parallel Structure

Parallel structure organizes items by their grammatical form. Items in the list must be all nouns, all adjectives, all infinitives, all prepositional phrases, all gerunds, or all clauses.

   Example: Tony likes *to eat, to drink,* and *to play.*

PRACTICE

Using parallel structure, add a word or phrase to finish each list.

Example: to talk, to run, and to sing

   1. to listen, to speak, and _____

   2. sleeping, rocking, and _____

   3. teachers, parents, and _____

   4. dog, cat, and _____

Rewrite each sentence to show parallel structure.

   Example: Benny sings, dances, and likes to act.
   Benny sings, dances, and acts.

1. Greg and Joe watched television, ate pizza, and went out to play football.

   _____

2. Amanda woke up, got dressed, and ran down the street to catch the bus.

   _____

3. The old house's windows were full of cracks, dirty, and broken.

   _____

4. The bicycle has large wheels, a seat that is big, and tall handlebars.

   _____

5. Make sure you stir the mixture, pour it into the pan, and are careful in smoothing it out.

   _____

6. The peacock's feathers were bright, shiny, and longer than most bird feathers.

   _____

WRITE ON!

On a separate sheet of paper, tell about items you would buy at a store. Make sure that the items in the list are in the same grammatical form.

Parallel Structure

Parallel structure organizes items by their grammatical form. Items in the list must be all nouns, all adjectives, all infinitives, all prepositional phrases, all gerunds, or all clauses.

    Example: Corrinne enjoys *laughing, singing,* and *dancing.*

PRACTICE

Underline the sentences that do not have parallel structure. Rewrite each sentence correctly on the lines.

Paragraph #1

Madge had an important presentation. To make sure everything went well, Madge read her notes, practiced her speech, and pretended to answer questions. When she felt ready, Madge walked up on the stage and took her place at the podium. After being introduced, Madge gave her speech, answered questions, and went to sit down. Madge did a great job.

_____

_____

Paragraph #2

Frisco and Emmett had been best friends since kindergarten. They liked the same sports, attended the same schools, and enjoyed eating the same foods. Their favorite sport was skateboarding. The boys rode their skateboards every chance they could get. On the weekends, their parents would find them at the skate park practicing flips, turns, and how to jump.

_____

_____

Paragraph #3

Gracie started her new job at the medical office. She was in charge of answering the phones, writing messages, and greeting the patients. When she had a spare minute, Gracie filed forms, updated charts, and put papers in the shredder. Gracie rarely had a free minute in her new job.

_____

_____

WRITE ON!

Do you have a best friend that you like to do things with? On a separate sheet of paper, write about your best friend and the things you enjoy doing together. Check each sentence to make sure parallel structure was used.

Name _____   Date _____

Transitional Words

Transitional words connect one sentence to the next and serve as a bridge from one paragraph to the next. There are many categories of transitional words: to compare, to add, to prove, to explain, to repeat, to show time, to show exception, to show sequence, to show emphasis, or to summarize or conclude.

Transitional Words of Comparison

after all	but	however	nevertheless	where
although	by comparison	in contrast	on the contrary	whereas
although this may be true	compared to	meanwhile	on the other hand	yet

PRACTICE

A Venn diagram is one way to jot down how two things are alike and different. Pick two items to compare. Write the name of one item on the left circle. Write the name of the other item on the right circle. The overlapped area is to show how the two items are alike. The separate circles are to list the difference. For guidance, see the example on the right.

WRITE ON!

On a separate sheet of paper, write a paragraph comparing the two items. Use transitional words of comparison in the paragraph, and underline them.

70

Name _____ Date _____

Transitional Words

Transitional words connect one sentence to the next and serve as a bridge from one paragraph to the next. There are many categories of transitional words: to compare, to add, to prove, to explain, to repeat, to show time, to show exception, to show sequence, to show emphasis, or to summarize or conclude.

Transitional Words of Sequence

after	before this	following this	second	subsequently
afterward	consequently	next	simultaneously	then
at this point	finally	now	so forth	third
at this time	first	previously	soon	therefore

Write the steps for doing a task. Use transitional words to connect one step to the next. Underline the transitional words used in the paragraph. For guidance, see the example below.

To wash a dog, <u>first</u> gather together all of the necessary items: tub, shampoo, old towels, comb or brush, large cup, and garden hose. <u>Second</u>, place the dog in the tub and, using the cup, begin gently prewashing the dog. <u>Third</u>, pour a generous amount of shampoo on the dog, and rub it into the dog's fur. <u>Fourth</u>, using the hose, rinse the dog. <u>Finally</u>, use the old towels to dry the dog, and comb out its fur.

_____
(Title of Topic)

_____

_____

_____

_____

_____

_____

_____

_____

_____

Without using sequential words, write about how you would make a peanut butter and jelly sandwich. Explain this on a separate sheet of paper. Exchange papers with a classmate. Ask the classmate to add the missing sequential words to the paragraph. Do you agree with the words your classmate chose?

Name _____   Date _____

Transitional Words

Transitional words connect one sentence to the next and serve as a bridge from one paragraph to the next. There are many categories of transitional words: to compare, to add, to prove, to explain, to repeat, to show time, to show exception, to show sequence, to show emphasis, or to summarize or conclude.

Transitional Words of Emphasis

absolutely	extremely	naturally	positively	unquestionably
always	in any case	never	surprisingly	without a doubt
certainly	in fact	obviously	undeniably	without reservation
definitely	indeed			

Think of a problem, issue, or idea that must be addressed in your community. (The problem, issue, or idea can be real or made-up.) Make a list of reasons why the problem needs to be addressed or idea implemented. Underline the transitional words used in the paragraph. For guidance, see the example below.

I must discuss an important problem that is showing up in our community. The problem is litter. Everywhere one goes, one can find litter where it does not belong: on the ground, in the streets, in people's yards. <u>Obviously</u>, this is a horrible problem that must be handled immediately. <u>In fact</u>, our community must organize a cleanup day to take care of this problem. <u>In any case</u>, each person must be a responsible citizen and make sure that he or she puts garbage in the garbage can and not on the ground.

_____
(Idea or Problem)

Reasons:

_____

_____

_____

_____

_____

_____

WRITE ON!

On a separate sheet of paper, write about a problem that must be addressed at your school. Use transitional words of emphasis in your paragraph, and underline them.

Name _____   Date _____

Transitional Words

Transitional words connect one sentence to the next and serve as a bridge from one paragraph to the next. There are many categories of transitional words: to compare, to add, to prove, to explain, to repeat, to show time, to show exception, to show sequence, to show emphasis, or to summarize or conclude.

Transitional Words of Time

after	finally	formerly	later	previously	soon	thereafter
and then	first	immediately	next	second	then	third

Tell about the events of the day. Underline the transitional words used in the paragraph. For guidance, see the example below.

Mrs. Jones went to the local farmer's market to purchase fresh fruits and vegetables. Mrs. Jones stopped at the first stand to purchase a bushel of corn. <u>After</u> that, Mrs. Jones went to the next stand and bought a basket of apples. <u>Then</u>, Mrs. Jones went to the watermelon stand and bought a big, juicy, ripe watermelon for the family. <u>Finally</u>, Mrs. Jones' shopping was done, and she returned home.

_____
(Title of Topic)

_____

_____

_____

_____

_____

_____

Without using transitional words, write about something a family member or pet did. What did the person (or pet) do first? Then, what happened? Write your answers on a separate sheet of paper. Exchange papers with a classmate. Ask the classmate to add the missing transitional words of time.

Name _____ Date _____

Sequential Order

Sentences, like directions, need to be written in **sequential order** so that the information makes sense to the reader.

Number the sentences in sequential order.

      Example: __2__ John filled out the information card.

            __1__ John took a pen out of his pocket.

            __3__ John put the pen back into his pocket.

            __4__ John turned in the card using both hands.

A. ____ Millie put air in the tire.

    ____ Millie had a flat tire.

    ____ Millie ran over a fork.

    ____ Millie patched the tire.

B. ____ The homeowner paid the painter.

    ____ The homeowner wanted his house painted.

    ____ The painter finished the job in three days.

    ____ The homeowner looked in the yellow pages for a painter.

C. ____ Write a letter to a friend.

    ____ Mail the letter.

    ____ Address the envelope, and put a stamp on it.

    ____ Fold the letter, and put the letter into the envelope.

On a separate sheet of paper, write the directions for doing a particular task out of sequence. Exchange papers with a classmate. Ask the classmate to number the sentences in sequential order.

Name _____   Date _____

Sequential Order

Sentences, like directions, need to be written in **sequential order** so that the information makes sense to the reader.

~~~ **PRACTICE** ~~~

Writing a story is like following a *recipe*.

- First, make a list of all the *ingredients* (or events, settings, and characters for the story).
- Then, decide which items need to be *added* (or written about) first.
- Finally, visualize what the finished *product* looks like (or how the story ends).

Write the steps for doing a specific task (making a bed, sharpening a pencil, etc.) or preparing a certain food (mac and cheese, a sandwich, etc.). After writing the steps, have a classmate act them out. Did you remember to include all of the steps? Are the steps in the correct order? Add any missing steps or renumber the steps so that they are in sequential order.

Make a list of the items to include in the directions: _____

_____

What should be done first? _____

_____

What will it look like when you are done? _____

Now, write out the directions for the task. Remember to include a title.

How to _____

_____

_____

_____

_____

_____

_____

_____

_____

~~~ **WRITE ON!** ~~~

On a separate sheet of paper, write the steps for getting from one point to another point within the classroom. Read the directions aloud, and ask a classmate to follow them. Were your directions correct?

Prefixes

A **prefix** is added to the beginning of a word to change its meaning.

Prefix	Meaning	Prefix	Meaning
ab–	away, from, off, not	mis–	wrong
auto–	self	mono–	one
bi–	two	pre–	before in place, time, rank, or order
cent–	hundred	re–	again, back
dis–	not, apart, away from	tri–	three
in–, im–, il–, ir-	not	uni–	one

PRACTICE

Use your knowledge of prefixes to determine the meaning of each word. Write each word's meaning on the line. (*Hint:* If you need help, use a dictionary.)

Example: redo: to do it again

1. absent: _____

2. unicycle:_____

3. centimeter: _____

4. pregame:_____

5. tricolor:_____

6. dishonest: _____

7. biceps: _____

8. misspell: _____

9. inactive: _____

10. preschool: _____

11. irresponsible:_____

12. illegal: _____

13. automobile: _____

14. impossible: _____

15. misfortune: _____

16. monotone: _____

17. refinish: _____

18. monolingual: _____

Read the paragraph. Underline the words with prefixes.

Bev and Stu went to the preshow at the local circus. At the preshow, Bev and Stu watched a clown ride a unicycle. He acted like he was going to fall and then regained his balance. Soon, a bear came out riding a bicycle. The bear clapped its paws, and its triplets came tumbling out on the stage. Each bear cub seemed to do the most impossible stunts ever. The first bear cub rode a tricycle. The second bear cub flexed its biceps before high-stepping across the stage. The third bear cub jumped on its mom's shoulders, disembarked, and returned to the center of the stage. It was quite a show!

WRITE ON!

Have you ever been to a circus or seen one on television? What kinds of things happened during the circus? Which animal act was your favorite? On a separate sheet of paper, write about the circus. Use prefixes in the paragraph, and underline them.

Name _____   Date _____

Suffixes

A **suffix** is added to the end of a word to change its meaning.

Suffix	Meaning	Suffix	Meaning
–er	one who	–est	superlative
–ness	state of being	–ful	full of
–ology	study of	–less	lack of, without
–or	one who	–ly	to what extent
–tion, –sion	action or process	–fy	to form into or become
–able, –ible	able to	–en	to make
–er	comparative		

PRACTICE

Use your knowledge of suffixes to determine the meaning of each word. Write each word's meaning on the line. (*Hint:* If you need help, use a dictionary.)

Example: teacher: one who teaches

1. frequently: _____

2. magnify: _____

3. kindness: _____

4. penniless: _____

5. joyful: _____

6. preparation: _____

7. edible: _____

8. confusion: _____

9. zoology: _____

10. tallest: _____

11. comfortable: _____

12. frighten: _____

13. meatless: _____

14. actor: _____

15. readable: _____

16. happiness: _____

Use your knowledge of suffixes to write the word described on the line.

1. the study of earth: _____

2. to be full of beauty: _____

3. to have the most money: _____

4. able to be liked: _____

5. to not have a head: _____

6. the process of discussing: _____

WRITE ON!

What would you do if you lost a shoe? Write your response on a separate sheet of paper. Use suffixes in the paragraph, and underline them.

Name _____ Date _____

Prefixes and Suffixes

A **prefix** is added to the beginning of the word to change its meaning.

   Example: *Retie* means to tie again.

A **suffix** is added to the end of the word to change its meaning.

   Example: *Tieless* means without a tie.

Prefix	Meaning	Suffix	Meaning
bi–	two	–er	one who
dis–	not, apart, away from	–ness	state of being
in–, im–, il–, ir–	not	–less	lack of, without
mis–	wrong	–able, –ible	able to
re–	again, back	–ful	full of

Use the prefixes and suffixes above to change the meaning of a base word. Write the new word and its meaning on the line. (*Hint:* If you need help, use a dictionary.)

   Example: cycle: bicycle: two wheels

1. fold: _____

2. turn: _____

3. possible: _____

4. deed: _____

5. allow: _____

6. taste: _____

7. bake: _____

8. gentle: _____

9. joy: _____

10. like: _____

On a separate sheet of paper, use five of the words in a paragraph. Exchange papers with a classmate. Ask the classmate to underline the words with prefixes and/or suffixes.

Name _____ Date _____

Latin Prefixes

A **prefix** is added to the beginning of a root word to change its meaning. A prefix cannot stand alone.

Latin Prefix	Meaning	Latin Prefix	Meaning
co–	together	post–	after
de–	away, off	pre–	before
dis–	not, not any	re–	again, back, backward
inter–	between, among	sub–	under
non–	not		

Use your knowledge of prefixes, as well as context clues from the surrounding words, to determine the underlined word's meaning in each sentence. (*Hint:* If you need help, use a dictionary.)

Example: Berta and Allie were appointed <u>cocaptains</u> of the team.

Meaning: They are leading the team together.

1. You can write a <u>postdated</u> check to pay for the merchandise.

Meaning: _____

2. This is a <u>nonissue</u>.

Meaning: _____

3. Use the <u>intercom</u> to call me when you are at the gate.

Meaning: _____

4. Mr. Thompson's work is <u>substandard</u> and will not meet the building code.

Meaning: _____

5. Her eyes widened in <u>disbelief</u>!

Meaning: _____

6. <u>Retrace</u> your footsteps to see if you can find the missing item.

Meaning: _____

7. Try to <u>prequalify</u> for the home loan.

Meaning: _____

8. Remember to <u>detach</u> the dog's leash when you are done walking him.

Meaning: _____

On a separate sheet of paper, write five other words that begin with a Latin prefix. Exchange papers with a classmate. Ask the classmate to write each word's meaning.

Name _____   Date _____

Latin Roots

A **root word** is part of a word. The root word has meaning by itself but cannot stand alone. The root word must have a prefix and/or a suffix added to it.

Latin Root	Meaning	Latin Root	Meaning
dict	to say	port	to carry
gress	to walk	scrib, script	to write
ject	to throw	tract	to pull, draw, move
pel	to drive	vert	to turn
pend	to hang		

PRACTICE

Use your knowledge of root words, as well as context clues from the surrounding words, to determine the underlined word's meaning in each sentence. (*Hint:* If you need help, use a dictionary.)

> Example: When one speaks, it is important to use clear <u>diction</u>.

> Meaning: to say things carefully

1. Put the incomplete work in the <u>pending</u> file.

   Meaning: _____

2. Use the <u>tractor</u> to do the heavy work on the farm.

   Meaning: _____

3. The bracelet can be <u>inscribed</u> with your name by any local jeweler.

   Meaning: _____

4. When the dog is through with its medication, it shall <u>revert</u> back to normal.

   Meaning: _____

5. The moving van will <u>transport</u> our belongings to our new home.

   Meaning: _____

6. The golfer <u>propelled</u> the ball through the air.

   Meaning: _____

7. What kind of <u>progress</u> are you making on the project?

   Meaning: _____

8. The girl <u>rejected</u> my offer to come with me to the dance.

   Meaning: _____

On a separate sheet of paper, write a paragraph on a topic of your choice. Use Latin root words in the paragraph, and underline them.

Name _____ Date _____

Latin Roots

A **root word** is part of a word. The root word has meaning by itself but cannot stand alone. The root word must have a prefix attached to the beginning of it and/or a suffix attached to the end of it to change its meaning.

Latin Prefix	Meaning	Latin Root	Meaning	Latin Suffix	Meaning
de–	away, off	dict	to say	–able, –ible	able to, capable, worthy of
dis–	not, not any	gress	to walk	–ion	makes a verb into a noun
inter–	between, among	ject	to throw	–fy, –ify	to make, cause to become
post–	after	pel	to drive	–ment	makes a verb into a noun
pre–	before	port	to carry	–ty	makes an adjective into a noun
re–	again, back, backward	scrib, script	to write		
sub–	under	tract	to pull, draw, or move		
trans–	across, beyond, through	vert	to turn		

Use your knowledge of prefixes, roots, and suffixes to write the meaning of each word on the line.

1. detract: _____
2. revert: _____
3. interjection: _____
4. postscript: _____
5. predict: _____
6. prescribe: _____
7. regress: _____
8. repel: _____
9. subtraction: _____
10. transport: _____

WRITE ON!

How can knowing Latin root words, prefixes, and suffixes help you when reading a passage or listening to information? Write your response on a separate sheet of paper.

Name _____ Date _____

Greek Prefixes

A **prefix** is added to the beginning of a root word to change its meaning. A prefix cannot stand alone.

Greek Prefix	Meaning	Greek Prefix	Meaning
a–, an–	without, not	mono–	one, single, alone
anti–, ant–	opposite, opposing	neo–	new, recent
auto–	self, same	pan–	all
bio–, bi–	life, living organism	thermo–, therm–	heat
micro–	small		

PRACTICE

Use your knowledge of prefixes to determine the meaning of each word. Write each word's meaning on the line. (*Hint:* If you need help, use a dictionary.)

Example: antisocial: not social

1. microscope: _____
2. pandemic: _____
3. autograph: _____
4. neoclassical: _____
5. biography: _____
6. thermometer: _____
7. biology: _____
8. monocle: _____
9. atypical: _____
10. panorama: _____

Underline the words with Greek prefixes used in the paragraph.

On our field trip, my class went to the museum in the city. The museum was built in a neoclassical style by the well-known artist, Flavia Timmons. As part of her design, microorganisms were engraved on the handrails. Ms. Timmons showed her interest in biology by using living plants as part of the landscape. When we climbed one of the many towers, we had a panoramic view of the museum and its surrounding land. Throughout the landscape, Ms. Timmons had monoliths carved from stone. Ms. Timmons did a fabulous job designing the museum.

WRITE ON!

On a separate sheet of paper, describe an item that can be found in a museum. Use words that have Greek prefixes in your paragraph.

Name _____ Date _____

DAILY Warm-Up 76

Greek Roots

A **root word** is part of a word. The root word has meaning by itself but cannot stand alone. The root word must have a prefix and/or a suffix added to it.

Greek Root	Meaning	Greek Root	Meaning
anthrop	human	path	feeling, suffering
chron	time	pedo, ped	child, children
dem	people	phon	sound
morph	form		

PRACTICE

Use your knowledge of root words, as well as context clues from the surrounding words, to determine the underlined word's meaning in each sentence. (*Hint:* If you need help, use a dictionary.)

Example: When I go to college, I can't wait to take a class on anthropology!

Meaning: study of humans

1. My dad always wears his chronometer on his left wrist.

   Meaning: _____

2. The United States is a democracy.

   Meaning: _____

3. My aunt has great empathy for people who are in pain.

   Meaning: _____

4. When I am sick, my mom takes me to the pediatrician.

   Meaning: _____

5. A phonograph is used to play vinyl records.

   Meaning: _____

6. In some music videos, people metamorphose into animals.

   Meaning: _____

7. An ape is an anthropoid because it is human-like.

   Meaning: _____

8. Make sure the events on the timeline are in chronological order.

   Meaning: _____

WRITE ON!

On a separate sheet of paper, write four new words with Greek roots in four different sentences. Exchange papers with a classmate. Ask the classmate to underline the words with Greek roots.

Name _____ Date _____

Greek Roots

A **root word** is part of a word. The root word has meaning by itself but cannot stand alone. The root word must have a prefix and/or a suffix added to it.

Greek Prefix	Meaning	Greek Root	Meaning	Greek Suffix	Meaning
a–, an–	without, not	anthrop	human	–ist	person who
anti–, ant–	opposite, opposing	chron	time	–gram	written or drawn, a record
auto–	self, same	dem	people	–graph	something written down, instrument for writing, drawing, or recording
bio–, bi–	life, living organism	morph	form	–logue, –log	speech, to speak
micro–	small	path	feeling, suffering	–meter, –metry	measuring device, measure
mono–	one, single, alone	pedo, ped	child, children	–oid	like, resembling shape or form
neo–	new, recent	philo, phil	love for	–phile	love for
pan–	all	phon	sound	–phobe, –phobia	fear of
thermo–, therm–	heat			–phone	sound, speaker of language, emits sound

PRACTICE

How many words can you make using the Greek prefixes, roots, and suffixes listed above? Write the words and their meanings on the line. (*Hint:* If you need help, use a dictionary.)

    Example: chronometer: something that measures time, like a watch

1. _____

2. _____

3. _____

4. _____

5. _____

WRITE ON!

On a separate sheet of paper, write a paragraph on a topic of your choice. Use Greek prefixes, root words, and suffixes in the paragraph, and underline them.

Name _____   Date _____

Greek Suffixes

A **suffix** is added to the end of a root word to change its meaning. A suffix cannot stand alone.

Greek Suffix	Meaning	Greek Suffix	Meaning
–ist	person who	–oid	like, resembling shape or form
–graph	something written down, instrument for writing, drawing, or recording	–phile	love for
–logue, –log	speech, to speak	–phobe, –phobia	fear of
–meter, –metry	measuring device, measure	–phone	sound, speaker of language, emits sound

PRACTICE

Use your knowledge of suffixes, as well as context clues from the surrounding words, to determine the underlined word's meaning in each sentence. (*Hint:* If you need help, use a dictionary.)

    Example: Chapter 11 is about <u>geometry</u>.

        Meaning: measure of shapes

1. Who was that on the <u>telephone</u>?

   Meaning: _____

2. The alien was <u>humanoid</u> in looks.

   Meaning: _____

3. My grandma was quite the <u>activist</u> when she was in college.

   Meaning: _____

4. What did they write in the first <u>telegraph</u>?

   Meaning: _____

5. In class, we watched a <u>travelogue</u> on India.

   Meaning: _____

6. How many <u>autographs</u> did you collect at the party?

   Meaning: _____

7. Do you have any <u>phobias</u>?

   Meaning: _____

8. My Uncle Jack is an <u>audiophile</u>.

   Meaning: _____

WRITE ON!

Are you an audiophile? Write about the kinds of things you like to listen to on a separate sheet of paper.

Name _____   Date _____

Etymology of Words—Spanish

Etymology refers to the history or origin of a word. Many words in the English language have their origins in the Spanish language.

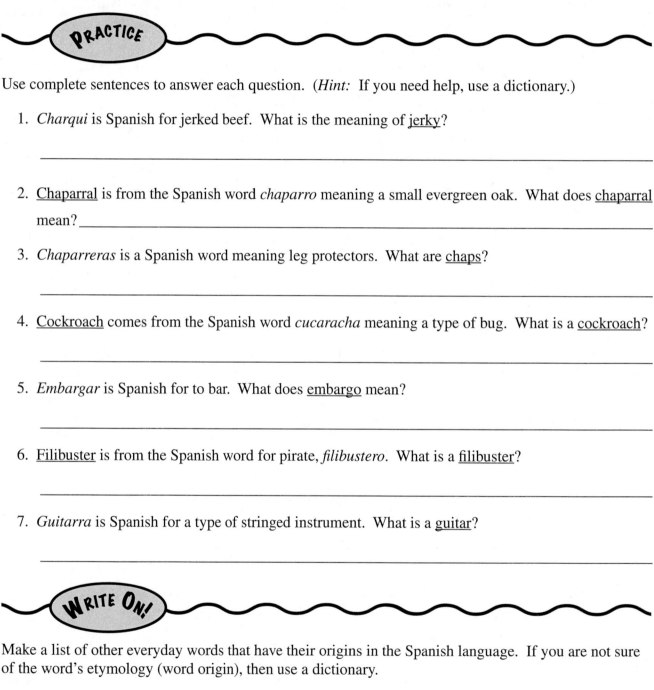

PRACTICE

Use complete sentences to answer each question. (*Hint:* If you need help, use a dictionary.)

1. *Charqui* is Spanish for jerked beef. What is the meaning of <u>jerky</u>?

   _____

2. <u>Chaparral</u> is from the Spanish word *chaparro* meaning a small evergreen oak. What does <u>chaparral</u> mean? _____

3. *Chaparreras* is a Spanish word meaning leg protectors. What are <u>chaps</u>?

   _____

4. <u>Cockroach</u> comes from the Spanish word *cucaracha* meaning a type of bug. What is a <u>cockroach</u>?

   _____

5. *Embargar* is Spanish for to bar. What does <u>embargo</u> mean?

   _____

6. <u>Filibuster</u> is from the Spanish word for pirate, *filibustero*. What is a <u>filibuster</u>?

   _____

7. *Guitarra* is Spanish for a type of stringed instrument. What is a <u>guitar</u>?

   _____

WRITE ON!

Make a list of other everyday words that have their origins in the Spanish language. If you are not sure of the word's etymology (word origin), then use a dictionary.

_____

_____

_____

Name _____ Date _____

Etymology of Words—French

Etymology refers to the history or origin of a word. Many words in the English language have their origins in the French language.

PRACTICE

Complete the chart. (*Hint:* If you need help, use a dictionary.)

French Word	Meaning	English Word	Meaning
1. avertissement	warning	advertisement	
2. avocat	attorney or lawyer	advocate	
3. ennuyer	to bother	annoy	
4. assumer	to take on	assume	
5. décomander	to cross out	cancel	
6. cap	land jutting out into the sea	cape	
7. croûte	crust	crouton	
8. dix	ten	dime	
9. fourchette	a type of pronged eating utensil	fork	
10. geste	movement	gesture	

WRITE ON!

Pick five of the English words with French origins. On a separate sheet of paper, use the words in a paragraph.

Name _____   Date _____

Etymology of Words—Hebrew

Etymology refers to the history or origin of a word. Some words in the English language have their origins in the Hebrew language.

PRACTICE

Use complete sentences to answer each question. (*Hint:* If you need help, use a dictionary.)

1. In Hebrew, *barukh haba* means blessed be the one who comes. What does <u>brouhaha</u> mean?

   _____

2. *Mevin* is Hebrew for one who understands. If someone is a <u>maven</u>, what does that mean?

   _____

3. In Hebrew, news or rumor is *shemu'oth*. What does <u>schmooze</u> mean?

   _____

4. In Hebrew, fit or acceptable is *kasher*. If something is <u>kosher</u>, what does that mean?

   _____

5. *Shabbat* means to rest in Hebrew. What is the <u>Sabbath</u>?

   _____

6. *Livyatan* means whale or sea monster in Hebrew. What is the meaning of <u>leviathan</u>?

   _____

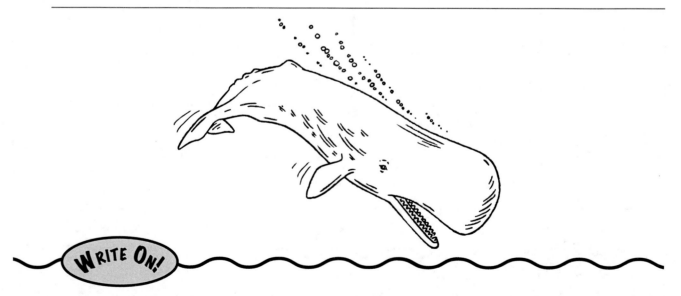

WRITE ON!

On a separate sheet of paper, use four of the words with Hebrew origins in sentences. Share the sentences with a classmate.

Name _____   Date _____

Etymology of Words—Irish

Etymology refers to the history or origin of a word. Some words in the English language are derivations of Irish words.

Read each Irish word and its meaning. Write the meaning for the English word below it. Then use each English word in a sentence. (*Hint:* If you need help, use a dictionary.)

1. *bean sidhe:* woman of the fairyland

    banshee: _____

    _____

2. *bogach:* wet or spongy ground

    bog: _____

    _____

3. *go leor:* plenty, a lot

    galore: _____

    _____

4. *fainne:* fake rings

    phoney:_____

    _____

5. *sluagh:* a large number, a great amount

    slew: _____

    _____

6. *smithers:* small pieces

    smithereens: _____

    _____

On a separate sheet of paper, write a paragraph on a topic of your choice. Use three of the words with Irish roots in the paragraph, and underline them.

Name _____   Date _____

Synonyms

Synonyms are two (or more) words that have the same or similar meaning.

Example: *Whining* and *complaining* are synonyms.

Write a synonym for each word. (*Hint:* If you need help, use a thesaurus.)

1. scoffed: _____

2. imagine: _____

3. authored: _____

4. ignorant: _____

5. considerate: _____

6. conceal: _____

7. respect: _____

8. suitable: _____

9. loyal: _____

10. unusual: _____

11. restored: _____

12. ignore: _____

13. thoughtful: _____

14. aware: _____

15. allowed: _____

16. agreed: _____

17. admire: _____

18. duty: _____

19. ordinary: _____

20. oppose: _____

Replace each underlined word with a synonym. Write the synonym on the line.

1. Toby has an <u>imaginary</u> friend named Skip.   _____

2. Jake <u>penciled</u> in his address.   _____

3. Who <u>authored</u> the story?   _____

4. Selena is a <u>polite</u> and thoughtful person.   _____

5. My dog is always <u>heedful</u> of the mail carrier.   _____

6. The garbage man <u>refused</u> my old sofa.   _____

7. Mom and Dad like to sit down and <u>discuss</u> issues.   _____

8. Would you like a <u>soft drink</u>?   _____

9. The spy was wearing a <u>disguise</u> when he was caught.   _____

10. Make sure the swimsuit that you wear is <u>appropriate</u> for school.   _____

On a separate sheet of paper, write four sentences. Underline one word in each sentence, and exchange papers with a classmate. Ask the classmate to write a synonym for each underlined word.

Name _____ Date _____

Synonyms

Synonyms are two (or more) words that have the same or similar meaning.

Example: *Barking* and *woofing* are synonyms.

Write two synonyms for each word. (*Hint:* If you need help, use a dictionary.)

Example: chair: seat, stool

1. size: _____ , _____

2. large: _____ , _____

3. soft: _____ , _____

4. teacher: _____ , _____

5. plant: _____ , _____

6. plate: _____ , _____

Read the paragraph. Replace each underlined word with a more interesting synonym. Write the synonym above the underlined word.

Bill and Mike were <u>riding</u> their bikes down the street. They decided to <u>stop</u> at the ice-cream shop and

get some ice cream. The boys <u>parked</u> their bikes and locked them to the bike rack. Bill and Mike

entered the cool ice-cream <u>shop</u> that had 50 flavors of ice cream.

"What can I do for you, boys?" <u>asked</u> the shop owner.

"Hmmm," <u>said</u> Bill. "I think I would like a scoop of vanilla ice cream."

"Coming right up," said the <u>man behind the counter</u>. "And, you, young man. What would you like?"

"I think I will have a scoop of vanilla ice cream and a scoop of chocolate ice cream," <u>said</u> Mike.

"Here you go, <u>boys</u>. Enjoy the ice cream."

"Thank you," <u>replied</u> both Bill and Mike.

What would you order at the ice-cream shop? On a separate sheet of paper, write a description of it two ways—using overused words and more interesting synonyms. Which paragraph is more fascinating to read?

Name _____ Date _____

Antonyms

Antonyms are two words that have opposite meanings.

Example: *Laughing* and *crying* are antonyms.

PRACTICE

Write an antonym for each word. (*Hint:* If you need help, use a thesaurus.)

1. rejects: _____
2. fancy: _____
3. healthy: _____
4. denies: _____
5. fear: _____
6. false: _____
7. broke: _____
8. whispered: _____

9. heavy: _____
10. bulky: _____
11. patient: _____
12. simple: _____
13. dull: _____
14. ordinary: _____
15. clumsy: _____
16. bore: _____

Replace each underlined word with an antonym. Write the antonym on the line.

Example: Today is the <u>happiest</u> day of my life!   _____saddest_____

1. Which student has the <u>neatest</u> desk? _____
2. Which color do you like the <u>most</u>? _____
3. I <u>always</u> do my homework. _____
4. This is the most <u>comfortable</u> couch in the world. _____
5. The parrot <u>screams</u> every time the doorbell rings. _____
6. My dog <u>found</u> his bone in the backyard. _____
7. The lawyer <u>won</u> her case. _____
8. The truck stopped at the <u>red</u> light. _____

Write two synonyms for each overused word.

1. bad: _____, _____
2. good: _____, _____
3. nice: _____, _____

WRITE ON!

On a separate sheet of paper, write a paragraph on a topic of your choice. Rewrite the paragraph replacing one word in each sentence with an antonym. Compare the two paragraphs. Do they convey the same meaning and tone?

Name _____ Date _____

Antonyms

Antonyms are two words that have opposite meanings.

Example: *Rich* and *poor* are antonyms.

PRACTICE

Write an antonym for each word. (*Hint:* If you need help, use a thesaurus.)

1. baby: _____
2. few: _____
3. unkept: _____
4. clammy: _____

5. together: _____
6. popular: _____
7. belittle: _____
8. hermit: _____

Rewrite the paragraph replacing each underlined word with an antonym.

Paragraph #1

Rebecca was so <u>excited</u>. She had <u>found</u> a raffle ticket on the ground. She knew that this was the <u>winning</u> ticket. The <u>first</u> prize was a gift certificate to the local computer store. With the gift certificate, Rebecca was going to buy a <u>new</u> digital camera. She kept her fingers crossed and hoped they would call out the raffle ticket's <u>numbers</u>.

_____

_____

_____

_____

Paragraph #2

Richie was so <u>dejected</u>. His team played their hearts out, but they still <u>lost</u> the game. What went <u>wrong</u>? Richie replayed the game over and over in his <u>mind</u>. Maybe if we had made that <u>last</u> basket, the game's outcome might have been different. Maybe if Benny had been on the <u>bench</u>, we might have stood a chance. Oh, well, next year's game might be different.

_____

_____

_____

_____

WRITE ON!

On a separate sheet of paper, write four sentences. Underline one word in each sentence. Exchange papers with a classmate. Ask the classmate to write an antonym for each underlined word.

Name _____ Date _____

Synonyms and Antonyms

Synonyms are two (or more) words that have the same or similar meaning.

    Example: *Pretty* and *beautiful* are synonyms.

Antonyms are two words that have opposite meanings.

    Example: *Pretty* and *ugly* are antonyms.

PRACTICE

Look at each pair of words. Are they synonyms (same meaning) or antonyms (opposite meaning)?
Write *synonyms* or *antonyms* on the line. (*Hint:* If you need help, use a dictionary.)

    Example: black, white _____antonyms_____

1. salty, sweet _____
2. friend, pal _____
3. eraser, pencil _____
4. thin, skinny _____
5. pasta, noodle _____
6. man, woman _____
7. tissue, hankie _____

8. shelter, house _____
9. brother, sister _____
10. change, coins _____
11. stereo, radio _____
12. sneaker, tennis shoe _____
13. gift, present _____
14. quiet, noisy _____

For each word, write a synonym and an antonym. (*Hint:* If you need help, use a thesaurus.)

	Synonym	**Antonym**
Example: hot	steaming	cold
1. hungry		
2. brave		
3. fierce		
4. spendthrift		
5. lost		
6. fast		
7. vegetarian		
8. careful		

WRITE ON!

What if there were no synonyms, only one word to express a feeling? What would it be like? Would
books be interesting to read? Would movies still be entertaining? Write your answers on a separate
sheet of paper.

Name _____ Date _____

DAILY
Warm-Up 88

Homographs

Homographs are words that are spelled the same but have different meanings and, sometimes, different pronunciations.

Example: address: where something is located, or to write a location on an envelope

PRACTICE

Write the two meanings for each word. Do the words have the same pronunciation? (*Hint:* If you need help, use a dictionary.)

Word	Meaning #1	Meaning #2	Same or Different Pronunciation
Ex. saw	to have seen	a tool used to cut wood	same
1. bass			
2. buffet			
3. dove			
4. number			
5. present			
6. record			
7. sewer			
8. use			
9. wind			
10. wound			

How do you determine the meaning of a homograph (or multiple-meaning word)?

_____

_____

WRITE ON!

On a separate sheet of paper, write five more homographs. Exchange papers with a classmate. Ask the classmate to write the two meanings for each word.

Name _____ Date _____

Homographs

Homographs are words that are spelled the same but have different meanings and, sometimes, different pronunciations.

Example: close: to shut, or marked by similarity in degree, action, feeling, etc.

Each homograph below has two meanings. Use each homograph in two sentences to show its different meanings.

Example: content: 1. something that is contained, 2. to be satisfied, happy

    1. I emptied the contents of the box onto the table.

    2. I am content with my lot in life.

A. contest: 1. to protest the outcome, 2. a game

    1. _____

    2. _____

B. defect: 1. a flaw, 2. to leave a country

    1. _____

    2. _____

C. entrance: 1. the opening to a building, 2. to delight

    1. _____

    2. _____

D. retract: 1. to take back, 2. to rewind

    1. _____

    2. _____

E. rose: 1. a type of flower, 2. got up

    1. _____

    2. _____

F. bow: 1. to bend at the waist, 2. a decorative knot

    1. _____

    2. _____

G. console: 1. to sympathize with someone else, 2. a small cabinet

    1. _____

    2. _____

On a separate sheet of paper, write a paragraph that contains three homographs. Ask a classmate to underline the homographs and, at the bottom of the page, write the meaning for each homograph.

Name _____ Date _____

Homographs

Homographs are words that are spelled the same but have different meanings and, sometimes, different pronunciations.

Example: desert: an arid region, or to leave without intending to return

PRACTICE

Circle the letter(s) of the sentences which correctly use the definition given for each homograph.

Example: arm: a body part

    a. A police officer carries a gun, mace, and an arm.

    (b.) My sister broke her arm when she fell out of a tree.

    c. Arm each soldier with a rifle, side arm, and a stun gun.

    (d.) An octopus has eight arms.

1. cab: a vehicle that transports people for money

    a. Cabs are often yellow.

    b. The pilot climbed into the cab of the plane.

    c. It's hard to find a cab in the rain.

    d. I couldn't believe how small the truck's cab was!

2. charge: to run full-speed at someone or something

    a. The football players charged the other team.

    b. The bull will charge his target.

    c. Percy can use his charge card at the hot dog stand.

    d. Vinnie charged his tuition and school books.

3. dip: a quick swim

    a. Zena likes to dip her toe into the pool.

    b. This is a great tasting dip.

    c. On hot days, I like to take a dip in the pond.

    d. Don't be such a dip!

4. duck: to lower one's head or body

    a. Make sure to duck when someone throws a ball at you.

    b. Some people eat duck soup.

    c. During an earthquake, duck under a desk or table.

    d. She will duck out as soon as possible.

WRITE ON!

Think of a homograph. On a separate sheet of paper, write the homograph and its two definitions. Ask a classmate to use the homograph in two sentences to show its two meanings.

Name _____ Date _____

Homographs

Homographs are words that are spelled the same but have different meanings and, sometimes, different pronunciations.

Example: dove: to have plunged into something, or a type of bird

Read the sentence. Circle the letter of the sentence that uses the underlined word in the same way as the first sentence.

Example: We made a <u>map</u> of the United States out of construction paper.
    a. The family will map out their trip to San Francisco.
    (b.) Fold the map and put it on the table.
    c. It's time for Tilly to map out a new career.

1. The <u>thunder</u> rumbled overhead.
    a. The train thundered down the tracks.
    b. During a storm, you might hear thunder and see lightning.
    c. My horse's name is Thunder.

2. The jack-in-the-box will <u>spring</u> out of the box when the lid is opened.
    a. There are many springs in the mattress.
    b. We will go fishing in the spring.
    c. The big, bad wolf likes to spring on unsuspecting pigs.

3. There is a sign on the <u>board</u>.
    a. My teacher is on the school board.
    b. The fence is made of boards.
    c. Did you see who was on the board?

4. My brother will go on a <u>mission</u>.
    a. Our class will visit the mission.
    b. The secret agent went on a mission.
    c. How many missions are in California?

On a separate sheet of paper, select a homograph, and use it in a sentence. Write three more sentences using the homograph and its different meanings. Exchange papers with a classmate. Ask the classmate to identify the sentence that uses the homograph in the same way as the original sentence.

Name _____ Date _____

Homographs

Homographs are words that are spelled the same but have different meanings and, sometimes, different pronunciations.

Example: polish/Polish: to make smooth and glossy, or the principal language of Poland

PRACTICE

Write the meaning for each homograph on the lines.

Example: <u>Mark</u> will place a <u>mark</u> beside each incorrect answer.

1. a person's name, 2. visible sign

1. Write your <u>name</u> at the top of the page, and then <u>name</u> ten animals that live in the ocean.

_____

_____

2. The movie about the winning baseball <u>hit</u> was a <u>hit</u> with all of the moviegoers.

_____

_____

3. My mom loves to <u>shop</u>, so she opened her own <u>shop</u> that sells collectible figurines.

_____

_____

4. Do you know how to <u>type</u> on this <u>type</u> of carbon paper?

_____

_____

5. I wrote a <u>paper</u> on how to make <u>paper</u> from scratch.

_____

_____

6. Do not <u>pet</u> my <u>pet</u> lion.

_____

_____

WRITE ON!

On a separate sheet of paper, name two ways to determine the meaning of a homograph. Which way is more accurate?

Homophones

Homophones are two or more words that sound the same but have different meanings and spellings.

>   Example: During the summer, the *air* is not healthy to breathe.

>   The *heir* to the throne is Prince Charming.

>   *Air* is something people breathe.

>   An *heir* is a person who inherits something from another person.

Underline the two homophones in each sentence.

>   Example: The <u>mail</u> carrier is a <u>male</u>.

1. So, you want to learn how to sew a quilt?

2. Be careful not to spill the flour all over the freshly cut flower.

3. Our marching band was banned from participating in the amateur competition.

4. Do you see how the sea waves rise and fall?

5. In this tale, the fox's tail gets stuck in the little pig's door.

6. Reading aloud is not allowed during the final test.

7. Some of the students figured out the correct sum.

8. My son jumps so high that he can almost reach the sun!

Write the meaning for each homophone.

1. sew: _____

2. flower: _____

3. sun:_____

4. some: _____

5. banned:_____

6. sea: _____

7. tale:_____

8. aloud: _____

How do you know which homophone to use in a sentence? On a separate sheet of paper, write a tip for others to use when writing homophones.

Name _____   Date _____

Homophones

Homophones are two or more words that sound the same but have different meanings and spellings.

Example: After working on my homework for three hours, I need to take a *break*.

In a car, you step on the gas to go and step on the *brake* to stop.

A *break* is a brief rest.

A *brake* is a device for slowing or stopping a vehicle.

Read the first sentence. Write a second sentence using the other homophone. Circle the homophone in the second sentence.

Example: The buzzing bumble <u>bee</u> flew back to its hive.

What do you want to (be) when you grow up?

1. I am pleased to <u>meet</u> your family.

_____

2. The blustery wind <u>blew</u> the house down.

_____

3. The scouts will collect some <u>wood</u> for the campfire.

_____

4. The farmer planted the vegetables in neat <u>rows</u>.

_____

5. Macy boiled water <u>to</u> make tea.

_____

6. The Williams stayed at the local <u>inn</u>.

_____

7. At <u>high</u> tide, all of the tide pools are filled with water.

_____

8. A <u>hare</u> is a rabbit.

_____

On a separate sheet of paper, write four sentences. Leave a blank line indicating where the homophone should go. Under the blank line, write the two homophones. Exchange papers with a classmate. Ask the classmate to circle the homophone that correctly completes each sentence.

Name _____ Date _____

Homophones

Homophones are two or more words that sound the same but have different meanings and spellings.

Example: My mood does *vary* every day.

I am *very* thankful to have friends and family.

Vary means to change or alter.

Very means to be extremely true.

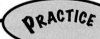

Circle the homophone that best completes each sentence.

Example: shear (sheer)   The _____ curtains are see-through.

1. their   there   Put the picture over _____.

2. stair   stare   It's not polite to _____ at strangers.

3. steal   steel   If you _____, then you might end up in jail.

4. tacks   tax   Hang up the artwork using _____.

5. loop   loupe   Many jewelers use a _____ to examine a gem's details.

6. shoe   shoo   What size _____ do you wear?

7. bare   bear   The tree is _____ of leaves.

8. two   too   I want to go, _____.

9. waist   waste   Put your trash in the _____ basket.

10. cent   sent   Grandma _____ the package via first class mail.

11. peace   piece   Would you like a _____ of pie?

12. buy   bye   Some people _____ everything they see.

13. pedal   peddle   When you _____ your bike, watch where you are going.

14. waive   wave   If you pay the entry fee early, they will _____ the parking fee.

15. warn   worn   I have _____ holes in the knees of all of my pants.

16. hall   haul   Sidney is the _____ monitor this week.

On a separate sheet of paper, write a paragraph on a topic of your choice. Use homophones in the paragraph, and underline them.

Name _____ Date _____

Idioms

An **idiom** is a word or phrase that cannot be interpreted literally. Instead, the word or phrase is a type of figurative language whose meaning is understood through common usage.

Example: It was a *blessing in disguise* that I missed the bus because it was involved in a major accident.

Meaning: At first, it seemed like the situation was a disaster, but in the end something good came from it.

Write the definitions next to their corresponding idioms.

Definitions	
finishing touch, something nice	to cross in the middle of the street, not at a crosswalk
to learn how to do something	to have patience
to slap another's hand in joy	to give the correct answer
something is always going wrong	to tell a secret
extremely quick passage of time	money set aside for retirement or emergencies

1. hit the nail on the head: _____

2. icing on the cake: _____

3. jaywalking: _____

4. New York minute: _____

5. if it's not one thing, it's another: _____

6. hold your horses: _____

7. nest egg: _____

8. high-five: _____

9. let the cat out of the bag: _____

10. learn the ropes: _____

Have you ever had a bad day where nothing seems to go right? On a separate sheet of paper, write about that day. Use idioms in the paragraph, and underline them.

Name _____ Date _____

Idioms

An **idiom** is a word or phrase that cannot be interpreted literally. Instead, the word or phrase is a type of figurative language whose meaning is understood through common usage.

Example: My mom got all *bent out of shape* when I showed her my math test.

Meaning: upset, angry, or irritated

Write the idioms next to their corresponding definitions.

Idioms	
backseat driver	beating around the bush
racing against the clock	chew someone out
crack someone up	down to the wire
blood is thicker than water	back to square one
cast-iron stomach	break a leg
cut to the chase	to cost an arm and a leg

1. to not be direct: _____

2. to be very expensive: _____

3. to be able to eat anything: _____

4. to tell someone else how to drive: _____

5. rushing to get a job done because there is limited time: _____

6. to yell at or berate another person: _____

7. family is more important than friends: _____

8. to have to start over: _____

9. to make someone laugh: _____

10. "good luck": _____

11. at the last moment: _____

12. get to the point: _____

How would you explain idioms to someone who is not a native speaker of English? Write your response on a separate sheet of paper.

Name _____ Date _____

Idioms

An **idiom** is a word or phrase that cannot be interpreted literally. Instead, the word or phrase is a type of figurative language whose meaning is understood through common usage.

    Example: What she said was *a slap in the face*.

    Meaning: an insult that causes disappointment

Complete each sentence with an idiom from the list below.

Idioms	
drives me up the wall	dry run
fuddy-duddy	everything but the kitchen sink
take sides	gave her her walking papers
get over it	don't count your chickens before they hatch
hit the hay	goes the extra mile
finger lickin' good	hit the books

1. My little brother is always bothering me. He _____.

2. Seth thinks he has the new job, but I told him _____.

3. The argument is over, so _____.

4. The students decided to _____ because they have a test tomorrow.

5. My sister is always late for work. Her boss finally _____.

6. The car comes with air-conditioning, a CD player, and _____.

7. Bob has worked a long day. He decided to _____ early.

8. My two best friends are fighting. I think I had better not _____.

9. The wedding consultant always _____ to make each wedding perfect.

10. The biscuits and gravy were _____.

11. Before we do the big show, we always do a _____.

12. Sometimes my dad can be such a _____.

Select one of the idioms to use in a paragraph describing your family as a whole or one family member. Write the paragraph on a separate sheet of paper.

Idioms

An **idiom** is a word or phrase that cannot be interpreted literally. Instead, the word or phrase is a type of figurative language whose meaning is understood through common usage.

> Example: Before I was invited to the dance, I felt *down in the dumps*.

> Meaning: sad

PRACTICE

What is the meaning of the underlined idiom?

1. Janet thought the job was <u>a piece of cake</u>.

    _____

2. The bully was given <u>a taste of his own medicine</u>.

    _____

3. Mark and his rude comments kept <u>adding fuel to the fire</u>.

    _____

4. We are <u>all in the same boat</u> since we didn't study for the test.

    _____

5. Jessica loses her temper at <u>the drop of a hat</u>.

    _____

6. Teddy <u>bends over backwards</u> to keep the customers happy.

    _____

7. Elisabeth <u>bit off more than she could chew</u> when she joined ten clubs.

    _____

8. Connor bought <u>a lemon</u> when he bought that clunker of a car.

    _____

9. Enrico always walks around with <u>a chip on his shoulder</u>.

    _____

10. Elise can't start her day without a <u>cup of joe</u>.

    _____

WRITE ON!

How do you think idioms come about? On a separate sheet of paper, write a paragraph explaining how you think idioms come into our everyday language.

Name _____   Date _____

DAILY
Warm-Up 100

Idioms

An **idiom** is a word or phrase that cannot be interpreted literally. Instead, the word or phrase is a type of figurative language whose meaning is understood through common usage.

    Example: Once I'm done with school, I want to make sure to *keep in touch* with my friends.

    Meaning: to stay in contact by phone, e-mail, etc.

PRACTICE

Underline the idioms in each paragraph. Then, rewrite the same paragraph replacing the idioms with plain, everyday language.

Paragraph #1

Brad had had a bad day. He had gotten off on the wrong foot with his teacher. He went up to ask the teacher a question, and, out of the blue, he sneezed all over the teacher. The teacher started to chew out Brad. Luckily, Brad was saved by the bell, and he was able to escape to his next class.

_____

_____

_____

_____

_____

Paragraph #2

Francine was so upset! Her brother broke her favorite CD, and all he was given was a slap on the wrist. Just because her little brother was the apple in her parents' eyes didn't mean he shouldn't be held accountable. Francine wanted to give her brother a taste of his own medicine. She ran into his room and looked around to see what she could break, but all he had were cardboard books and stuffed animals. Francine decided to get over it and went to watch cartoons with her brother.

_____

_____

_____

_____

_____

_____

WRITE ON!

Which paragraphs are more interesting to read? Why? Write your response on a separate sheet of paper.

Name _____ Date _____

Similes

A **simile** compares two things using the words *like* or *as*. A simile describes a person or item in a colorful, interesting way.

Example: She is *as mad as a wet hen.*

Meaning: angry

Underline the simile in each sentence.

1. My dad is as strong as an ox.
2. Her stomach rumbled like thunder.
3. Gerald laughs like a hyena.
4. She looks like she just rolled out of bed.
5. Paula's skin is as white as snow.
6. Without my glasses, I am as blind as a bat.
7. The baby is as cute as a button.
8. You look like you've been through a war.
9. Tina looks like a fish out of water.
10. Her breath smells like a fresh mint.
11. The carpenter was as busy as a beaver.
12. The bathroom is as clean as a whistle.
13. Her mind is like a computer.
14. Eddie runs around like a hamster in a wheel.
15. Gina is as happy as a clam.
16. Kate is as hungry as a bear.
17. My kitty roars like a lion.
18. She eats like a bird.

Complete each simile.

1. I am stuffed _____ .
2. We are _____ .
3. Elliot is _____ .

On a separate sheet of paper, write four similes. Share them with a classmate.

Name _____ Date _____

Similes

A **simile** compares two things using the words *like* or *as*. A simile describes a person or item in a colorful, interesting way.

    Example: My mom is *as explosive as a volcano*.

    Meaning: temperamental

PRACTICE

Underline the simile in each sentence. Write its meaning on the line.

1. Cassie is like a bull in a china shop.

   Meaning: _____

2. Jed runs like the wind.

   Meaning: _____

3. Brad is as proud as a peacock.

   Meaning: _____

4. Her eyes are as bright as a new penny.

   Meaning: _____

5. Ingrid looks like the cat who ate the canary.

   Meaning: _____

6. Wally is as nimble as a monkey.

   Meaning: _____

7. Jackie eats like a bird.

   Meaning: _____

8. They fought like two weasels in a bag.

   Meaning: _____

9. Her directions were as clear as mud.

   Meaning: _____

10. Bella is as light as a feather.

    Meaning: _____

WRITE ON!

Use a simile in each sentence describing the contents of your desk. Write these on a separate sheet of paper. Underline each simile.

Name _____ Date _____

Similes

A **simile** compares two things using the words *like* or *as*. A simile describes a person or item in a colorful, interesting way.

Example: She is *as happy as a clam.*

Meaning: very happy and content

Read the paragraphs. Underline the similes.

Paragraph #1

The building stood tall like a mountain. With the antenna on its top, it looked like a missile getting ready for take off. The windows were as shiny as aluminum foil. It was a wonder to behold.

Paragraph #2

The afternoon was as hot as a sauna, but it was as cool as a refrigerator in the shade. Leo decided to take a snooze in the hammock that was tied to two large shade trees. Soon, Leo was snoring like a buzz saw as the hammock rocked him like a baby.

Paragraph #3

The tiny mouse peeked from its hole and then ran as quick as a wink across the cat's whiskers. The cat took off after the mouse. The little mouse gave a squeak as loud as a lion's roar. The mouse used its tail like a whip and snapped it across the cat's nose. The cat's nose felt as burned as lit firewood. The little mouse made it safely back to its home.

Paragraph #4

The boy was so angry. It looked like steam was coming from his ears. He stomped his feet like a bull getting ready to charge. He whipped his head to the right and to the left. He rolled his hands into fists as big as boulders and shook them in the air. He was as angry as a rattlesnake.

On a separate sheet of paper, describe a time when you were feeling strong emotions—happiness, sadness, anger, joy. Make sure to include similes in your response. Exchange papers with a classmate. Ask the classmate to underline the similes.

Name _____ Date _____

Metaphors

A **metaphor** compares two things but does not use the words *like* or *as*. A metaphor describes a person or item in a colorful, interesting way.

Example: Shannon is *pricklier than a cactus in bloom.*

Meaning: difficult to get along with

What is the meaning of each metaphor?

1. It is hotter than a sauna!

   Meaning: _____

2. Jen is a walking encyclopedia of facts and information.

   Meaning: _____

3. I need a crane to lift my dog.

   Meaning: _____

4. The leaves were graceful dancers in the wind.

   Meaning: _____

5. Mrs. Greene is luckier than a four-leaf clover on St. Patrick's Day.

   Meaning: _____

6. Her fingers were all thumbs when playing the piano.

   Meaning: _____

7. She gave a shark's smile before answering the question.

   Meaning: _____

8. His smelly feet made the skunks turn tail and run.

   Meaning: _____

9. Jake's thick head could be mistaken for a brick wall.

   Meaning: _____

10. Her brain was a sandstorm of ideas.

    Meaning: _____

On a separate sheet of paper, use several metaphors to describe yourself, a family member, or a pet.

Name _____   Date _____

DAILY
Warm-Up 105

Metaphors

A **metaphor** compares two things but does not use the words *like* or *as*. A metaphor describes a person or item in a colorful, interesting way.

> Example: She was *jumping with joy* at the good news.

> Meaning: extremely happy

PRACTICE

What is the meaning of each metaphor?

1. It is raining cats and dogs.

   Meaning: _____

2. In this neck of the woods, life runs at a slower pace.

   Meaning: _____

3. Jenna is the apple of her dad's eye.

   Meaning: _____

4. Diane was just a twinkle in her dad's eye during the Great Depression.

   Meaning: _____

5. Mike Moneybags is rolling in the dough.

   Meaning: _____

6. My mom is dead tired after working all day.

   Meaning: _____

7. Mrs. Gurney was a wet blanket at her grandson's party.

   Meaning: _____

8. When it comes to food, my brother has a hollow leg.

   Meaning: _____

9. She danced with two left feet.

   Meaning: _____

10. Kevin was boiling mad after missing that last shot during the game.

    Meaning: _____

WRITE ON!

On a separate sheet of paper, use metaphors to describe the condition of your desk or your bedroom. Share your metaphors with a classmate.

Figurative Language

Name _____ Date _____

Metaphors

A **metaphor** compares two things but does not use the words *like* or *as*. A metaphor describes a person or item in a colorful, interesting way.

    Example: The judge's decision was *difficult to swallow.*

    Meaning: The person didn't like the decision the judge made.

Underline the metaphors used in the paragraphs.

Paragraph #1

The baby was positively sunny! She gurgled and chortled as the family showered her with attention, hugs, and kisses. When she became tired, her big sister rocked her to sleep. When she tried to remove the baby's pacifier, she found it cemented in the baby's mouth.

Paragraph #2

The football player leapt with a ballerina's grace into the air to catch the football. He landed softer than a cloud on one foot and thundered down the field to score the winning touchdown. The football player spiked the football and raised his fist in victory!

Paragraph #3

Babe found the homework to be a breeze. She blasted through the math assignment and then glided through the spelling. When Babe finished her homework, she decided to make brownies. She stirred the mixture in a frenzy of anticipation. Then, she licked her lips as the brownies baked. At her first bite, Babe thought she tasted a bit of heaven.

Write a metaphor to describe the following events.

    1. A happy birthday: _____

    2. A hard test: _____

    3. Winning a contest: _____

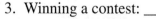

On a separate sheet of paper, write a short paragraph about an event. Now, rewrite the paragraph using metaphors in one or two of the sentences. Which paragraph is more interesting to read?

Name _____ Date _____

Similes and Metaphors

A **simile** compares two things using the words *like* or *as*.

　Example:　She is *as slow as a snail.*

A **metaphor** compares two things but does not use the words *like* or *as*.

　Example:　Tina can be *such a mule* if she doesn't get her way.

PRACTICE

Decide if each sentence contains a simile or a metaphor.　Write your answer on the line.

　Example:　Vince was boiling mad after locking his keys in the car.　　　____metaphor____

1. Greta froze in fear when faced with the rampaging bull.　　　_____

2. Sarah's voice was music to his ears.　　　_____

3. Alma was as pretty as a picture in her prom dress.　　　_____

4. Her smile could light up the world.　　　_____

5. Her muscles could bend steel.　　　_____

6. In the heavy coat, she looked like a pig in a blanket.　　　_____

7. The dog's teeth were as sharp as nails.　　　_____

8. He drove like a madman through the busy city streets.　　　_____

9. Nick is down in the dumps.　　　_____

10. The chair swiveled like a merry-go-round.　　　_____

11. Susie's memory is cloudy about the events of the day.　　　_____

12. The discussion ended on a sour note.　　　_____

13. Her taste in clothing is a cry for help.　　　_____

14. The chili burned a hole in my stomach.　　　_____

15. The night was like a dream.　　　_____

16. His voice was like a foghorn.　　　_____

17. The fire burned like an inferno.　　　_____

18. All of the men wore their penguin suits to the formal event.　　　_____

WRITE ON!

On a separate sheet of paper, explain the difference between a simile and a metaphor.　Share your explanation with a classmate.

Name _____ Date _____

Analogies

An **analogy** consists of two pairs of words. In each pair of words, the first word is related in some way to the second word. In solving an analogy, first determine the relationship between the first pair of words. Are the words synonyms, antonyms, part-whole, cause and effect, etc.? Then, use the same relationship to complete the second pair of words.

Examples: hot : cold

This is read as "hot is to cold." The relationship is *opposites*.

hot : cold :: young : old

This is read as "hot is to cold as young is to old."

Both pairs of words describe a relationship of *opposites*.

PRACTICE

Complete the analogies. Use the same relationship from the first pair of words to complete the second pair of words.

Example: apple : fruit :: carrot : vegetable

1. fingers : body :: checkers : _____

2. spoon : silverware :: table : _____

3. wheel : bike :: engine : _____

4. ill : sick :: healthy : _____

5. scrub : clean :: bald : _____

6. exhausted : tired :: giggle : _____

7. up : down :: left : _____

8. cursive : printing :: throw : _____

9. open : closed :: tight : _____

10. pencil : write :: straw : _____

11. ruler : measure :: telephone : _____

12. eyeglasses : see :: hearing aid : _____

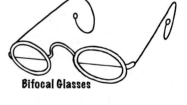

Bifocal Glasses

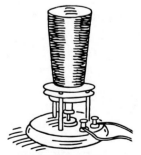

First Hearing Aid

WRITE ON!

On a separate sheet of paper, write four analogies. Exchange the analogies with a classmate. Ask the classmate to identify the relationship between each pair of words.

Name _____ Date _____

Analogies

An **analogy** consists of two pairs of words. In each pair of words, the first word is related in some way to the second word. In solving an analogy, first determine the relationship between the first pair of words. Are the words synonyms, antonyms, part-whole, cause and effect, etc.? Then, use the same relationship to complete the second pair of words.

Examples: stove : cook

This is read as "stove is to cook." The relationship is *cause and effect*.

stove : cook :: fireplace : heat

This is read as "stove is to cook as fireplace is to heat."

Both pairs of words describe a relationship of *cause and effect*.

PRACTICE

Complete each set of analogies. Identify the relationship.

	Analogy	**Relationship**
1. teeth : chew :: ears :	_____	_____
2. numbers : count :: letters :	_____	_____
3. bus : road :: airplane :	_____	_____
4. bread : toast :: egg :	_____	_____
5. salt : pepper :: up :	_____	_____
6. Sunday : day :: February :	_____	_____
7. happy : smile :: sad :	_____	_____
8. feet : legs :: hands :	_____	_____
9. puppy : dog :: kitten :	_____	_____
10. one : odd :: two :	_____	_____

Write two analogies of characteristic.

Example: cloud : soft :: iron : hard

1. _____

2. _____

WRITE ON!

On a separate sheet of paper, write four analogies. Rewrite the analogies leaving out one of the words. Exchange incomplete analogies with a classmate. Ask the classmate to complete the analogies. Compare the classmate's analogies to the original analogies.

Name _____   Date _____

Analogies

An **analogy** consists of two pairs of words. In each pair of words, the first word is related in some way to the second word. In solving an analogy, first determine the relationship between the first pair of words. Are the words synonyms, antonyms, part-whole, cause and effect, etc.? Then, use the same relationship to complete the second pair of words.

    Examples: giddy : excited

          This is read as "giddy is to excited." The relationship is synonyms.

          giddy : excited :: irate : anger

          This is read as "giddy is to excited as irate is to anger."

          Both pairs of words describe a relationship of synonyms.

PRACTICE

Write an analogy for each category.

Example: Cause and effect: rain : flood :: snow : avalanche

  1. Part to whole: _____

  2. Whole to part: _____

  3. Synonym: _____

  4. Antonym: _____

  5. Specific item to its general category: _____

  6. Object to its action: _____

  7. Object to its material: _____

  8. Object to its definition: _____

  9. Offspring to adult: _____

10. Object to its description: _____

11. Object to color: _____

12. Relationship: _____

WRITE ON!

On a separate sheet of paper, name four different analogy relationships. Exchange papers with a classmate. Have the classmate write an analogy that fits each relationship.

Name _____ Date _____

DAILY
Warm-Up 111

Dictionary

A **dictionary** is a reference book. A dictionary contains a list of words in alphabetical order. A dictionary usually provides the following for each entry word:

- syllabication
- pronunciation
- part of speech
- definition
- sample usage in a sentence
- derivations of the word

PRACTICE

Write each list of words in alphabetical order.

1. astronaut, agriculture, age, asteroid, agony, agent, assemble, aghast, asterisk, assignment

_____, _____, _____, _____, _____,

_____, _____, _____, _____, _____,

2. jumbo, juniper, Jupiter, June, jumping, junction, jungle, judge, juror, junk

_____, _____, _____, _____, _____,

_____, _____, _____, _____, _____,

3. church, child, chip, chomp, chicken, chilly, chintz, cheap, chime, chimney

_____, _____, _____, _____, _____,

_____, _____, _____, _____, _____,

4. rooster, robot, romance, rocketry, Roman, romper, roast, rosette, royal, rodeo

_____, _____, _____, _____, _____,

_____, _____, _____, _____, _____,

5. mandarin, mannequin, mantle, Manchurian, maniac, manual, mange, manager, manuscript, mannerly

_____, _____, _____, _____, _____,

_____, _____, _____, _____, _____,

WRITE ON!

Why is it important that the words in a dictionary are arranged in alphabetical order? Write your response on a separate sheet of paper.

Name _____ Date _____

Dictionary

A **dictionary** is a reference book. A dictionary contains a list of words in alphabetical order. At the top of each dictionary page are the guide words. The guide words tell the first and last words on that particular page.

Examples: ape–banana

Ape will be the first entry word on the page.

Banana will be the last entry word on the page.

Any other words that fit alphabetically between the two guide words will be found on that particular page.

PRACTICE

Write each list of ten words in alphabetical order. Then, write two possible guide words for the dictionary page that they would appear on.

1. poodle, pompom, pomegranate, post, polygraph, police, pooch, pork, polar, pollinate

Guide Words: _____ – _____

_____, _____, _____, _____, _____,

_____, _____, _____, _____, _____

2. newspaper, newsworthy, notes, nautical, naughty, nose, noisy, numb, noteworthy, newscast

Guide Words: _____ – _____

_____, _____, _____, _____, _____,

_____, _____, _____, _____, _____

Use a dictionary to look up two of the words from above, and fill in the chart.

Word	Part of Speech	Pronunciation	Syllables	Definition	Derivations

WRITE ON!

Pretend that you have a friend who has never heard of a dictionary. On a separate sheet of paper, describe a dictionary and its uses to your friend.

Name _____ Date _____

Dictionary

A **dictionary** is a reference book. A dictionary contains a list of words in alphabetical order. A dictionary also provides the correct spelling (or spellings) for a given word.

Look at the list of words below. Use a dictionary to determine which words are spelled correctly and which ones are spelled incorrectly. If the word is spelled correctly, place a checkmark in the box. If the word is spelled incorrectly, write the correct spelling of the word in the box.

Word	Correct Spelling
Example: a lot	✔
1. vacum	
2. beeleve	
3. bellwether	
4. truely	
5. dumbell	
6. ocasionaly	
7. greatful	
8. embaras	
9. mispell	
10. neighbor	
11. priviledge	
12. recieve	
13. rythm	
14. libary	

Write two words that always give you spelling trouble. Can you think of a way to help you remember the correct spelling?

     Example: raccoon   Raccoon has two *os* that look like eyes.

1. _____

2. _____

Which is better to use—a dictionary or spell check? Why? Write your response on a separate sheet of paper.

Name _____   Date _____

Dictionary

A **dictionary** is a reference book. A dictionary contains a list of words in alphabetical order. A dictionary also provides the pronunciation for each word.

Look at each pair of words. Which one shows the correct pronunciation? Circle the correct answer. When in doubt, look up the word in the dictionary.

Word Choice #1	Word Choice #2
assessory	accessory
dialate	dilate
sherbet	sherbert
espresso	expresso
upmost	utmost
irregardless	regardless
library	libary
miniature	miniture
heigth	height
mischievious	mischievous
probly	probably
realtor	realator
excape	escape
Febyuary	February

Write three words that you frequently mispronounce or that you frequently hear mispronounced and the correct pronunciation for each word.

Mispronounced Correct Pronunciation

1. _____   _____

2. _____   _____

3. _____   _____

On a separate sheet of paper, write a paragraph on a topic of your choice. Deliberately mispronounce several of the words in writing. Exchange papers with a classmate. Ask the classmate to circle the mistakes in the paragraph.

Name _____   Date _____

Glossary

A **glossary** is a dictionary that is located in the back of a book. A glossary contains vocabulary that is specific to that book's topic.

Look in three books with glossaries. Record the following information.

Title of Book	Type of Book (textbook, reading book, non-fiction, science, etc.)	Information Contained in the Glossary (pronunciation guide, definition, word usage, pictures, etc.)	Vocabulary in Book (How are the words shown in the book—boldfaced, highlighted, italics, etc.)

On a separate sheet of paper, write about a special talent, hobby, or skill that you have. Underline the special vocabulary used in the paragraph. On the back of the page, make a glossary showing the special vocabulary used in the paragraph.

DAILY
Warm-Up 116

Thesaurus

A **thesaurus** is a reference book. A thesaurus provides synonyms for a given word. Some thesauruses also provide antonyms (opposites) for a word. A thesaurus can be used to find new or unusual words to convey a specific meaning. Using a variety of words can also make one's writing more interesting to read.

Examples: It was a *cold* night, so I put on a *jacket*.

It was a *chilly* night, so I put on a *parka*.

Which sentence makes you feel shivery just reading it?

PRACTICE

Write three synonyms for each word. (*Hint:* If you need help, use a thesaurus.)

Example: cap: hat, bonnet, helmet

1. cold: _____ , _____ , _____

2. blanket: _____ , _____ , _____

3. picture: _____ , _____ , _____

4. light: _____ , _____ , _____

5. creature: _____ , _____ , _____

6. cage: _____ , _____ , _____

Rewrite each sentence using a synonym to replace the underlined word.

1. The <u>boat</u> was large and luxurious.

   _____

2. A <u>person</u> scribbled all over the walls.

   _____

3. I want a <u>dog</u> that is fluffy, large, and smart.

   _____

WRITE ON!

On a separate sheet of paper, make a list of ten words that you use all of the time in writing or speaking. Now, look up synonyms for those words in the thesaurus. Write a synonym next to each overused word.

DAILY
Warm-Up 117

Thesaurus

A **thesaurus** is a reference book. A thesaurus provides synonyms for a given word. Some thesauruses also provide antonyms (opposites) for a word. A thesaurus is great for expanding one's vocabulary and for finding alternatives to overused words.

Example: Bill likes to drink *cold* water.

Bill likes to drink *icy* water.

PRACTICE

Write three synonyms for each word. (*Hint:* If you need help, use a thesaurus.)

Example: old: vintage, antique, heirloom

1. scratched: _____ , _____ , _____

2. old: _____ , _____ , _____

3. cuddly: _____ , _____ , _____

4. shining: _____ , _____ , _____

5. delicate: _____ , _____ , _____

Rewrite each sentence replacing the underlined word with a synonym from above.

1. The <u>old</u> dresser belongs to my great, great-grandparents.

   _____

2. The <u>scratched</u> record made a horrible sound on the record player.

   _____

3. The <u>cuddly</u> teddy bear belongs to the baby.

   _____

4. In Hollywood, everyone thinks he or she is a <u>shining</u> star.

   _____

5. The delivery person brought a <u>delicate</u> package.

   _____

WRITE ON!

On a separate sheet of paper, write a sentence. Rewrite the sentence two more times replacing the commonly used words with synonyms. Compare the three sentences. Which one is the most interesting to read?

Name _____ Date _____

Thesaurus

A **thesaurus** is a reference book. A thesaurus provides synonyms for a given word. Some thesauruses also provide antonyms (opposites) for a word. A thesaurus can provide alternate word choices to replace overused words. This will make your writing more interesting to read.

Example: Jeni likes to lay out in the *hot* sun.

Jeni likes to lay out in the *sweltering* sun.

To make the following paragraphs more interesting to read, draw a line through overused words, and replace them with synonyms. Write the synonyms above the overused words.

Paragraph #1

My aunt is a police officer. Each shift she puts on her blue uniform, shines her yellow badge, and

polishes her shoes. Around her waist, my aunt wears a belt. The belt contains all of her gear, like

handcuffs, a baton, and mace. When she is all dressed, my aunt drives her clean patrol car to the station

to begin her shift.

Paragraph #2

The quiet student read a book. The book was good. When the student finished reading the book, he

put the book back into his backpack. The student took out a notebook and pencil and began writing a

paragraph about the book that he had read.

Paragraph #3

My dog likes to chew on dog bones, any kind of dog bones. My dog likes big bones and crunchy bones.

His favorite bones are the giant-sized ones that the butcher gives him. The bones look like they came

from a big dinosaur. My dog will chew on the giant-sized bone all day.

On a separate sheet of paper, write a paragraph about something interesting, odd, or humorous that an animal has done. The animal can be a pet, a zoo animal, or an animal in a television commercial. Add zip to the paragraph by using interesting words.

Name _____   Date _____

Card Catalog

A **card catalog** is located in the library. A card catalog sorts information about a book into three categories: title, author, and subject. Each card in the card catalog contains bibliographic information about the book (author, publisher, publication date) as well as multiple cross-references. Information contained on each card in the card catalog includes:

- Author's name, including pseudonyms
- Publication information
- Number of pages in the book
- Type of illustrations, charts, photos
- Cross-reference materials

PRACTICE

Use the card catalog to look up the same book title three different ways: by title, author, and by subject. Record the information you find.

Title Card	
Author Card	
Subject Card	

Were there any differences in the information shown on the three different cards?

_____

_____

WRITE ON!

Besides the card catalog, how else could all of the books in the library be inventoried? Write about your system on a separate sheet of paper.

Name _____ Date _____

Dewey Decimal System

Melvil Dewey created a system for cataloging books in a library. Each book in the library has a call number. The call number has two parts: the Dewey Decimal Classification number and the Cutter number.

- The Dewey Decimal number places the book into one of ten categories. (*Note:* Only eight categories are shown below.) Each category is then divided into subcategories.

- The Cutter number consists of the first letter of the author's last name, followed by a series of numbers that keep the book in alphabetical order by the author's last name.

- A work mark or work letter sometimes follows the final number in the Cutter number. The work mark or work letter is a lowercase letter that is usually the first letter of the title of the book. This helps to distinguish books by the same author.

Examples: 590.00 (Dewey Decimal number)

R1234 (Cutter number)

798g (Work mark or Work letter)

PRACTICE

Select a library book from each Dewey Decimal category below. Record the following information.

Dewey Decimal Category	Dewey Decimal Number	Book Title	Author's Last Name	Topic
000				
100				
200				
300				
400				
500				
600				
700				

WRITE ON!

On a separate sheet of paper, write a paragraph describing the Dewey Decimal System of cataloging books.

Name _____   Date _____

Dewey Decimal System

Melvil Dewey created a system for cataloging books in a library. Each book in the library has a call number. The call number has two parts: the Dewey Decimal Classification number and the Cutter number.

- The Dewey Decimal number places the book into one of ten categories. Each category is then divided into subcategories.
- The Cutter number consists of the first letter of the author's last name, followed by a series of numbers that keep the book in alphabetical order by the author's last name.
- A work mark or work letter sometimes follows the final number in the Cutter number. The work mark or work letter is a lowercase letter that is usually the first letter of the title of the book. This helps to distinguish books by the same author.

Examples: 590.00 (Dewey Decimal number)

R1234 (Cutter number)

798g (Work mark or Work letter)

PRACTICE

Find two books by the same author. Record the following information.

Author	Book Title	Dewey Decimal Number	Cutter Number	Work Mark or Work Letter

Pick one of the books from above. Find two other books with the same Dewey Decimal number.

Book Title	Call Number (Dewey Decimal Number and Cutter Number)

WRITE ON!

Is the Dewey Decimal System easy to use? Why? Write your response on a separate sheet of paper.

Name _____ Date _____

Dewey Decimal System

The **Dewey Decimal System** has ten main categories. Each category is divided into ten subcategories.

PRACTICE

Find a book for each of the eight subcategories shown below. Write the book title and the entire call number in the box. Then, answer the questions below using the chart.

500 Science and Mathematics			
	SubCategory	**Book Title**	**Call Number**
500	Natural Science		
510	Mathematics		
520	Stars, Planets, Astronomy		
530	Physical Science (force, motion, electricity, magnetism, etc.)		
540	Chemistry, Atoms, Molecules		
550	Volcanoes, Earthquakes, Weather		
560	Dinosaurs, Prehistoric Animals		
570	Forests, Deserts, Mountains, Oceans, Evolution		

1. If you wanted to find out more about hurricanes, where would you look? _____

2. If you needed help in Math, where would you look? _____

3. If you wanted to find out more about Jupiter, where would you look? _____

4. If you found a book about electricity, where would you shelve the book? _____

5. If you wanted to find out which mountain is the tallest, where would you look? _____

WRITE ON!

Pretend you work at a library. What would be your most important task? Why? Write your response on a separate sheet of paper.

Name _____ Date _____

Dewey Decimal System

The **Dewey Decimal System** is a way of organizing and classifying books in a library. Books are shelved by topic and can be located by their call number.

Biographies tell about a person's life. Under the Dewey Decimal System, the biographies are all shelved together. The Cutter number is assigned to the biographee (who the book is about). A second Cutter number is for the author or editor of the biography.

> Examples: 900 (Biography)
>
> B62 (*B* stands for biographee's last name)
>
> D85 (*D* stands for author or editor's last name)

Some books come out yearly. Each year's edition is shelved by the year of publication.

> Examples: 030 (Encyclopedia)
>
> 1984 (year published)

PRACTICE

Write the name of one person you would like to learn more about. Use the card catalog to find three different books about that person. Write the title and call number for each book.

Person: _____

Book Title: _____ Call Number: _____

Book Title: _____ Call Number: _____

Book Title: _____ Call Number: _____

Visit the reference section of the library. Write the titles and call numbers for three different reference books that contain information about this person.

Book Title: _____ Call Number: _____

Book Title: _____ Call Number: _____

Book Title: _____ Call Number: _____

WRITE ON!

On a separate sheet of paper, write a paragraph describing the library (school or public). What things can be found in the library besides books?

Name _____   Date _____

Library of Congress Classification System

The Library of Congress contains almost every book ever published in the United States. The **Library of Congress Classification System** is used in many large libraries. The system has twenty classes (or categories) of books. Letters are used to identify each class of books.

Library of Congress Classification System	
A–General Works	N–Fine Arts
B–Philosophy, Psychology, and Religion	P–Language and Literature
C-F–History	Q–Science
G–Geography, Anthropology, Recreation	R–Medicine
H–Social Sciences	S–Agriculture
J–Political Science	T–Technology
K–Law	U–Military Science
L–Education	V–Naval Science
M–Music	Z–Bibliography and Library Science

PRACTICE

Identify each book's category. Write the correct corresponding letter on each line.

1. Modern dance: _____

2. Biography on Coldplay: _____

3. Laws of Hawaii: _____

4. Periodic table: _____

5. United States Army: _____

6. Democratic Government: _____

7. The Civil War: _____

8. History of computers: _____

9. Crops of the southwest: _____

10. Foreign language dictionary: _____

11. Teaching kids how to read: _____

12. An almanac: _____

13. Maps of the United States: _____

14. Ancient man: _____

15. Exercising for fun: _____

16. Viruses and diseases: _____

17. Taking care of livestock: _____

18. Navy: _____

19. A favorite sports team: _____

20. Developing photographs: _____

WRITE ON!

Which system do you think is easier to use—The Dewey Decimal System or the Library of Congress Classification System? Why? Write your response on a separate sheet of paper.

Name _____   Date _____

Periodical Index

A **periodical** is an ongoing publication, such as a magazine, newspaper, or journal.

PRACTICE

Make a list of titles for each type of periodical. (*Hint:* If you need help, visit the library.)

Magazines—These are popular periodicals that contain a variety of topics. Magazines also have pictures and contain advertising.

    1. _____

    2. _____

    3. _____

Serials—These are annuals and yearbooks.

    1. _____

    2. _____

    3. _____

Trade and Professional Journals—These are aimed at a specific audience and contain a specialized vocabulary.

    1. _____

    2. _____

    3. _____

News Magazines—These provide factual information on different topics.

    1. _____

    2. _____

    3. _____

Newspapers—Newspapers might be published daily or weekly. They contain up-to-date information on current events.

    1. _____

    2. _____

    3. _____

WRITE ON!

Which type of periodical do you read? What kinds of information does the periodical contain? Write your responses on a separate sheet of paper.

Name _____   Date _____

Periodical Index

A **periodical** is an ongoing publication, such as a magazine, newspaper, or journal. To find an article in a periodical, use a periodical index. A periodical index lists articles by subject or by author.

The **periodical index** contains information about the article. This information is called a citation. The citation includes:

- Author or editor's name
- Article title
- Title of the periodical

- Volume and issue number (Journals only)
- Date of the periodical's issue
- Pages the article can be found on

Example: Sause, Bob. "Teach your bulldog new tricks." <u>You and Your Bulldog</u> 20 Nov. 2007: 24–28.

PRACTICE

Write the citations for three articles from different types of periodicals.

1. _____

    _____

    _____

2. _____

    _____

    _____

3. _____

    _____

    _____

WRITE ON!

Develop a magazine cover on a separate sheet of paper. Include the title of the magazine, volume and issue number, date of publication, as well as some articles and page numbers that can be found in the magazine. Exchange magazine covers with a classmate. Ask the classmate to write a citation for one of the articles shown on the cover of the magazine.

Name _____   Date _____

Citing Sources—Bibliography

Citing a source means giving credit to the person or organization who developed the idea, found the information, or made the statement (quotation). All of the material used to do the report is included in the report's bibliography. The bibliography is located on the last page of the report. Use the chart below as a guide to citing sources.

Books	Articles	Web Sites	Electronic Resources
Author or editor's name	Author or editor's name	Author or editor's name	Author or editor's name
Title of book	Title of article	Title of article	Database name or title of the project, book, or article
Publication city	Title of periodical	Title of periodical	Any version numbers available
Publisher Year	Volume and issue number (Journals only)	Publication date	Date of version, revision, or posting
	Publication date	Date of access	Publisher information
	Page numbers	Web site address (URL)	Date of access
			Web site address (URL)

PRACTICE

Write a citation for each source of information. An example has been provided for both types.

Book

Smith, Jan. <u>Fashion for Life,</u> New York: Penguin, 2008.

_____

_____

Web site

<u>Clothes for All Seasons</u>. 26 Aug. 2007. The TCR School of Fashion. 11 July 2008 <www.clothesforallseasons.com>.

_____

_____

WRITE ON!

Why is it important to give credit to the source of the information? Write your response on a separate sheet of paper.

Name _____   Date _____

Citing Sources—Footnotes

A **footnote** cites a source for information. The footnote is located at the bottom of the same page that the information was presented. Each footnote is numbered sequentially throughout the report, starting with the number 1.

Example: 3. Joe Pastore. <u>Leisurely Weekend</u>, New York: Scribner, 2004.

Notice that the author's name is listed with the first name first and the last name last. This is the reverse of what is used in a bibliography.

PRACTICE

Look in several textbooks to find footnotes. Write three footnotes from the textbooks below.

Footnote #1: _____

_____

Footnote #2: _____

_____

Footnote #3: _____

_____

Look in the bibliography section for each of the textbooks. How are these same informational sources listed in the bibliography? Write the citations below.

Bibliography Source #1: _____

_____

Bibliography Source #2: _____

_____

Bibliography Source #3: _____

_____

WRITE ON!

On a separate sheet of paper, explain the difference between a footnote and a bibliography.

Name _____ Date _____

Colons

- Use a **colon** before listing a series of words that follow a complete sentence.

    Example: Babies need many things: diapers, clothes, toys, shoes, and formula.

- Use a **colon** to separate two complete sentences. When doing so, the first letter of each part of the sentence is capitalized.

    Example: The rules are simple: No personal phone calls or e-mails while on the job.

Add a colon to each sentence. Add capitalization whenever it is necessary.

1. There is no such thing as a free puppy puppies need vet care, food, toys, and treats.

2. Taking care of your smile is easy brush and floss your teeth each day.

3. The tree's bark was scraped, branches were broken, and food was missing the wild cat had struck again.

4. Everybody must wear the school uniform shirts, pants, socks, and ties.

5. We made many projects in arts and crafts class coffee mugs, dinner plates, and vases.

6. I know how Abigail earned an A on her test she copied Amber.

7. The car was packed with kids, suitcases, snacks, and the family dog Seattle, here we come!

8. Campers must follow the rules to be safe in the mountains clean up trash, put out the campfire, and store food in the metal lockboxes.

9. The food was cold Mario missed dinner again.

10. In order to get a good night's sleep, Penny has to have her stuffed animals Sadie, Figaro, Vigo, and Zeta.

What are the rules at your school? Are they fair? Write your response below. Remember to use a colon when needed.

_____

_____

_____

Name _____ Date _____

Colons

- Use a **colon** to separate a title from its subtitle.
  Example: *How to Eat All You Want: Diet Tips for Everyone*

- Use a **colon** to show time.
  Example: The train leaves at 3:15 p.m.

- Use a **colon** after a salutation in a business letter.
  Example: Dear Sir:

- Use a **colon** to separate the place of publication and the publisher.
  Example: Los Angeles: Tompkins Publishing, 1982.

- Use a **colon** to cite a law.
  Example: Education Code 32:259 states that no child may wear licorice in his or her hair.

Underline the words or numbers that need a colon. Write the underlined words or numbers correctly on the line.

    Example: School is dismissed at <u>205</u> p.m.   <u>2:05 p.m.</u>

1. My first book *Red and Purple More Than Just Colors* is about my life. _____
2. Mona's dental appointment is at 1045 a.m. _____
3. The book's citation read Chicago Farm Hands Publishing, 2009. _____
4. *How to Boil Water A Cookbook for Beginners* is a fabulous cookbook. _____
5. We had lunch at 1130 a.m. _____
6. The police code 10 21B means "to call home." _____
7. *Mothers They Are Always There* is a great Mother's Day gift. _____
8. "A female motorist needing help" is an 11 25X. _____
9. The auction ended at 400. _____
10. Does the matinee start at 320? _____
11. The letter began, "Dear Sir I have a complaint to register." _____
12. The kids were cited for breaking law 11 15: Playing ball in the street. _____
13. Section 25 087 in the Education Code has to do with excused absences. _____
14. The book *Being Green Twelve Easy Steps* is about saving our planet. _____

On a separate sheet of paper, write the rules for using a colon. Share the rules with a classmate.

Punctuation

Name _____   Date _____

Semicolons

There are three uses for a semicolon.

- Use a **semicolon** in place of a coordinating conjunction when combining two complete sentences that are related.

    Example: Sue went to the store; Margaret went home.

- Use a **semicolon** before a conjunctive adverb that joins two independent clauses (or two complete sentences). A comma follows the conjunctive adverb. Conjunctive adverbs are: *accordingly, afterwards, also, consequently, however, indeed, likewise, moreover, nevertheless, nonetheless, similarly, still,* and *therefore.*

    Example: I left my shopping list at home; consequently, I forgot several items.

- Use a **semicolon** to separate items in a series if the items already contain commas.

    Example: Ned bought three pairs of high-top sneakers; a pair of tan, baggy pants; four dressy shirts; and a necktie.

Add semicolons and commas to the following sentences.

    Example: Jerry broke his collarbone; his brother set it for him.

1. Christopher is in room six his twin brother is in room seven.

2. Montel is on television he anchors the morning news.

3. My dog was barking up a storm it wanted me to rub its belly.

4. Nancy wants to be a school psychologist however her parents want her to be an engineer.

5. The doorbell rang nobody answered it.

6. The children were naughty with the babysitter therefore they had to go to bed early.

7. James finished his report he gave it to the teacher.

8. Marty carefully folded the towels, sheets, and blankets cleaned the windows, floors, and baseboards and straightened the cushions, seat covers, and throw pillows.

9. Bertha learned how to ride a unicycle still she is afraid of losing her balance on it.

10. Anne just graduated from nursing school therefore she will be looking for a job.

11. Billy practices the piano every day he plays very well.

12. Stu runs several miles each morning consequently he is in great shape.

On a separate sheet of paper, write three sentences to illustrate how and when to use a semicolon.

Name _____ Date _____

Quotation Marks

Quotation marks are used to show what a person said.

- The first word within the quotation marks is capitalized.
    Example: "Everyone knows what happened," said Doug.

- Use a comma before starting the quotation.
    Example: Mom asked, "What happened?"

- Put commas and periods within the quotation marks.
    Example: "Dad," said my brother, "we had a food fight."

Add quotation marks to sentences where the person's exact words are used.

Example: Dad said, "Let's go to the museum."

1. Mom said that we could go to the mall.
2. Turn to page twenty-four in your science books, said Mrs. Plumb.
3. The anchor reported that the team lost the game after going into overtime.
4. Stop by the cafeteria, and see our amazing display of student artwork, announced the principal.
5. It was an accident, said Madge.
6. Look out! screamed Nadia.

Read the dialogue. Put quotation marks around each speaker's exact words.

Zack was excited about the opening of the new skate park. Hey Josh! Let's head over there and get some air time! he said.

Sounds good to me, replied Josh. The two boys grabbed their boards and walked across the street to the skate park.

I can't wait to try the big ramp! said Josh.

Me, too, said Zack. I have also been wanting to try out the wall.

Watch this! screamed Josh. He rode his board off the ramp and did a somersault in midair.

Whoa! That was amazing! said Zack.

On a separate sheet of paper, write a dialogue between you and your parent or you and your friend. Remember to use quotation marks around each person's exact words.

Name _____ Date _____

Quotation Marks

- Use **quotation marks** for the titles of short works, such as songs, short stories, essays, short poems, and one-act plays.

    Example: The poem, "How Do I Love Thee," is often read at weddings.

- Use **quotation marks** for chapters in a book, articles in a newspaper or magazine, and episodes of television and radio.

    Example: I read the "How to Make Friends" chapter from the book *Friends Are Everywhere.*

- Use **quotation marks** when quoting poetry. A slash mark indicates the end of a poetry line.

    Example: "How many ways can I help you?/Let me bring you up when you are feeling blue."

Read the paragraph, and add the missing quotation marks.

For the Peach Blossom Festival, our class read the poem, Follow the Teacher. The recitation started off strong. The boys started the poem with, We were following the teacher/And talking to each other, and then Bryce fell off the stage! Carly and the rest of the class went to help him back up.

Bryce, are you okay? asked Carly.

Bryce was a bit woozy and started singing Wheels on the Bus but soon forgot the words.

I am okay, said Bryce, but maybe we can start the poem over.

The judges let the class start over, and they did a bang-up job.

Next time, said Bryce, I will be more careful about where I am standing. The whole class laughed.

Write three chapter titles and the books they can be found in. Remember to use quotation marks when writing the chapter titles.

_____

_____

_____

_____

_____

140

Name _____   Date _____

Apostrophes

An **apostrophe** is used for two reasons:

- To make a noun possessive
   Example: This is Jan's house.

- To take the place of omitted letters in a contraction
   Example: are + not = aren't (The missing letter is *o*. The apostrophe takes its place.)

PRACTICE

Rewrite each sentence to show possession using an apostrophe.

   Example: Dave has a green bike.   _____ Dave's bike is green. _____

   1. Mary has the big chair.   _____

   2. The pilot of the plane enjoys flying.   _____

   3. Steve has a black boom box.   _____

   4. This passport belongs to Garth.   _____

   5. Stan will have a birthday next week.   _____

Write the contraction for each pair of words.

   1. does not _____   11. would not _____

   2. she will _____   12. I have _____

   3. is not _____   13. I am _____

   4. do not _____   14. will not _____

   5. they are _____   15. they will _____

   6. they had _____   16. has not _____

   7. he is _____   17. you are _____

   8. you will _____   18. we are _____

   9. we have _____   19. could not _____

   10. could have _____   20. should have _____

WRITE ON!

On a separate sheet of paper, write about your friend's favorite breakfast food. Check to make sure you used each apostrophe correctly.

Name _____   Date _____

Apostrophes

An **apostrophe** is used for two reasons:

- To make a noun possessive

    Example: This is Bailey's food.

- To take the place of omitted letters in a contraction

    Example: do + not = don't (The missing letter is *o*. The apostrophe takes its place.)

PRACTICE

Underline the words that need an apostrophe. Then, rewrite the paragraph correctly.

Kate travels the world looking for unique items for her familys store and for customers. Last week, Kate flew to Spain to look at rugs. In Luis rug store, Kate found the perfect rug for the Sandovals house. The colors were beautiful. Luis said that the blue in the rug matched Kates eyes perfectly. Kate bought the rug and asked Luis to ship the rug to the Sandovals.

_____

_____

_____

_____

_____

Karis doctor tells people its easy to avoid getting sick. The doctor says to wash ones hands with soap and water several times each day. Soap doesnt allow germs to multiply and spread. The doctor also says dont drink from someone elses cup. This wont let germs transfer from one person to another. Follow the doctors advice, and you wont get sick this year.

_____

_____

_____

_____

WRITE ON!

What is the best advice you have ever been given or the best advice that you have given to someone else? What was the outcome of the advice? Write your response on a separate sheet of paper. Use apostrophes in your sentences, and underline them.

Name _____ Date _____

Commas

A **comma** is used to separate two independent clauses (or complete sentences) that are joined with a coordinating conjunction (*for, and, nor, but, or, yet, so*).

    Example: Mark washed the car, *and* he took out the garbage.

        Mark washed the car is an independent clause.

        *He took out the garbag*e is an independent clause.

PRACTICE

Add a comma to the sentences that combine two independent clauses.

    Example: Grace washed her hands, and she loaded up the dishwasher.

1. I thought I left my glasses here but I can't find them.

2. It was time for the play to start but the cast was not ready to go onstage.

3. Henry was extremely thirsty so he drank some water.

4. Pam went to the grocery store and the dry cleaners.

5. The printer doesn't work so I called a repairperson.

6. The cable car couldn't stop so the people jumped out of its way.

7. Paul left his jacket at home so I let him borrow mine.

8. The telephone was dropped yet it still works.

9. The lawn needs to be mowed and the leaves need to be raked.

10. She won the water gun war but not by much.

11. Joan is running for treasurer for she is good with money.

12. My parrot loves to eat seeds and sing songs.

Write three pairs of complete sentences joined with a coordinating conjunction.

    1. _____

    2. _____

    3. _____

WRITE ON!

If you were to go bird-watching, what would you expect to see? What kinds of things would you need to take with you? Write your response on a separate sheet of paper. Use coordinating conjunctions in your paragraph, and underline them.

Name _____ Date _____

Commas

A **comma** is used when a dependent clause begins a sentence. The comma goes between the dependent clause and the independent clause (or main sentence). Some common words that introduce dependent clauses are *after, although, as, because, if, since, when,* and *while*.

> Example: While I was eating dinner, a ball went whizzing through the kitchen window.
>
> *While I was eating dinner* is a dependent clause. A comma is used to separate it from the main sentence.

PRACTICE

Add a comma when a dependent clause begins a sentence. If a dependent clause does not begin a sentence, do not add a comma.

> Example: After the bell rang, five students walked through the classroom door.

1. Because it was out of gas the car wouldn't start.
2. After the party was over we all went to Dave's house.
3. The phone rang while everyone was gone.
4. After we eat dinner let's play tag.
5. When you hear the whistle blow start running.
6. The camera wouldn't work after it was dropped on the ground.
7. Open the windows when the weather is nice.
8. If the grass is dry it needs more water.
9. As soon as Jim gets here we can head off to the mountains.
10. The music is loud because the volume is turned up.
11. Plug in the cell phone because the battery needs to be recharged.
12. Since it is so hot why don't we all head to the local swimming pool?

Write three sentences with dependent clauses. Use commas as needed.

1. _____

2. _____

3. _____

WRITE ON!

Has your alarm clock ever failed to go off? Did it make you late for school or for an appointment? Write about the experience on a separate sheet of paper.

Name _____ Date _____

Commas

- Use a **comma** after introductory phrases. An introductory phrase is not a complete sentence because it does not have both a subject and a verb.

  Examples: To get a seat at the concert, you need to get to the stadium early.

  After lunch, I will go exercise.

- Use a **comma** after introductory words. Common introductory words are *well, yes, still, furthermore, meanwhile*, and *however.*

  Examples: Yes, I would like to go to the concert with you.

  However, I think the punishment does not fit the crime.

PRACTICE

Underline and add a comma after each introductory phrase or introductory word.

1. In the middle of the night the door squeaked open.

2. Crying crankily the baby finally fell asleep.

3. Well here comes Mr. Iverson.

4. Meanwhile we all sat in our seats waiting for the speech to begin.

5. Still it's about time you started looking for a job.

6. After directing a film Tabitha McNeery visited our acting company.

7. Furthermore more students are deciding to go to college than into the work force.

8. Feeling sick Jan decided not to go to school.

9. Making up his mind Jeremy ordered a hamburger.

10. To look at houses on the market Roger called a real estate agent.

Write two sentences with introductory phrases.

1. _____

2. _____

Write two sentences with introductory words.

1. _____

2. _____

WRITE ON!

Pretend you had to introduce a famous author, celebrity, or sports figure to your class. What would you say? Write your speech on a separate sheet of paper. Use introductory phrases or words, and underline them.

Name _____ Date _____

Commas

Use a **comma** when listing a series of three or more events or items. The comma takes the place of the word *and*. Use a comma with the final *and* in the series of events or items. (*Note:* A comma can also take the place of *or*, if it is being used to list a series of events or items.)

    Example: Marge ate a hamburger and a hot dog and a pretzel and an ice-cream cone.

                 Marge ate a hamburger, a hot dog, a pretzel, and an ice-cream cone.

PRACTICE

Rewrite each sentence. Add commas when needed.

    Example: Gracie chased the ball and drank some water and ran after the cat.

                 Gracie chased the ball, drank some water, and ran after the cat.

1. Would you like a glass of lemonade or water or milk or iced tea?

    _____

2. Nina invited Seth and Bob and Ben and Trina and Maggie to her party.

    _____

3. Sam packed shirts and pants and socks and shoes for his trip to Maine.

    _____

4. Katie can't find her purse or wallet or keys.

    _____

5. The Sorensons visited five states: New York and Pennsylvania and New Jersey and Maryland and Virginia.

    _____

6. This semester, Al is taking physics and calculus and poetry and Spanish.

    _____

7. On Saturday, we can go to the water park or the amusement park or the bowling alley.

    _____

8. While camping, we saw squirrels and moose and owls and bears.

    _____

WRITE ON!

On a separate sheet of paper, write about a time that you were offered a choice of things to do. Which one did you pick? Why? Use commas in your sentences, and underline them.

Name _____ Date _____

Commas

- Use two **commas** to set off nonessential clauses in the middle of a sentence. A nonessential clause can be removed from the sentence, and the meaning of the sentence is unchanged.

    Example: My sister, who is older than I, went to Harvard.

- Use a **comma** to separate the date from the year.

    Example: November 26, 2009

- Use a **comma** to separate the city from the state.

    Example: Tulare, California

- Use a **comma** before a direct quotation.

    Example: Mom said, "Dinner is ready!"

Use two commas to set off the nonessential clause in each sentence.

    Example: Barney, the Labrador retriever, ate the entire plate of bacon!

1. Heather who enjoys reading edits children's books.

2. Bugsy whose real name is Bogart likes to act like he's big and tough.

3. The mug which is made from glass is full of hot coffee.

Write two sentences with nonessential clauses.

1. _____

2. _____

Add the missing commas to the paragraph.

Visalia California, a small town in the Central Valley is my hometown. I was born on July 30 1980,

at the local hospital. My mother after bringing me home from the hospital could not believe how

little I was. She said "This is the tiniest baby I have ever seen!" Well, she could not say that for

long because I ate and ate and ate and ate!

On a separate sheet of paper, write a brief autobiography about a certain time in your life. It could be as a newborn, a toddler, or a young child. Check to make sure commas were used correctly in the paragraph.

Name _____   Date _____

Capitalization

- Use a **capital letter** when writing the first word in a sentence.

    Example: Who ate the last piece of cake?

- Use a **capital letter** when writing the pronoun *I*.

    Example: Bill and I went mountain climbing.

- Use a **capital letter** when writing the names of proper nouns (specific people, places, organizations, and things).

    Examples: Mrs. Johnson, Supreme Court, The Boys and Girls Club, Fresno, CA

PRACTICE

Rewrite each sentence with correct capital letters.

    Example: mel went to the eye doctor.

        Mel went to the eye doctor.

1. my family spent summer vacation in orlando, florida.

    _____

2. trina and betty are best friends.

    _____

3. have you ever eaten at daisy's restaurant?

    _____

4. we went back-to-school shopping at bennet's department store.

    _____

5. which case went to the supreme court?

    _____

6. clay gave a wonderful speech about honesty.

    _____

7. my car, the red viva, gets wonderful gas mileage.

    _____

8. my parakeets, bailey and luna, love to take baths.

    _____

WRITE ON!

On a separate sheet of paper, write about a pet you have or one you would like to have. Check to make sure capital letters were used correctly in the paragraph.

Capitalization

- Use a **capital letter** when writing the first letter of a family member's name if it is being used as a proper noun.

    Example: Mom and Dad are having a party.

    (*Hint:* If you can substitute a name in place of *Mom* or *Dad*, then *Mom* or *Dad* are proper nouns and need to be capitalized.)

- Use a **capital letter** when writing the first letter(s) of a job title that comes before a name.

    Example: Mayor Dill runs the city of Clovis.

- Use **capital letters** when writing words in a title, except for prepositions, articles, and coordinating conjunctions. (Exception: If a preposition, article, or coordinating conjunction is the first word of a title, then capitalize it.)

    Example: "The Most Important Day of My Life" (title of a poem)

PRACTICE

Underline the word or words that should be capitalized. Write the word or words correctly on the line.

Example: <u>aunt sue</u> lives in <u>pennsylvania</u>.   _____Aunt Sue, Pennsylvania_____

1. let's throw a party for my mom and my dad!   _____

2. did you get to meet coach henson?   _____

3. grandma and grandpa live in exeter, California.   _____

4. "learning to love school" is a great article.   _____

5. judge alexander presides over criminal cases.   _____

6. uncle bill is a police officer in austin, texas.   _____

7. my brothers and sisters have all attended the local college.   _____

8. *the Hardest times make the best Memories* is my favorite book.   _____

9. sergeant evans visits many classrooms in schools.   _____

10. *the time it takes to listen* is an interesting play.   _____

11. the cabin belongs to my aunts and uncles.   _____

12. my neighbor, professor marx, teaches history at the local college.   _____

WRITE ON!

On a separate sheet of paper and without using any capital letters, write a paragraph about specific people in your life. Make sure to include a title at the top of the page. Exchange papers with a classmate. Ask the classmate to underline the words that should be capitalized.

Name _____   Date _____

Capitalization

- Use a **capital letter** when writing the first letter of a direction that names a region of the country. (Do not capitalize the first letter of a compass direction.)

    Example: The Perrys have moved to the Northeast.

- Use a **capital letter** when writing the first letter of a day of the week, month of the year, and holiday.

    Example: The first day of the week is Sunday.

PRACTICE

Underline the word or words that should be capitalized. Write the word or words correctly on the line.

    Example: My aunt lives in west texas.   _____West Texas_____

1. Do you like fridays or sundays better?   _____

2. february is the shortest month of the year.   _____

3. My best friend moved to west orange county.   _____

4. labor day is in september.   _____

5. My favorite months are june, july, and august.   _____

6. Tabitha lives in the pacific northwest.   _____

7. mother's day is in may.   _____

8. There are four mondays in this month.   _____

9. My cousin grew up in south chicago.   _____

10. When is independence day?   _____

Use complete sentences to answer the following questions.

1. When is your birthday? _____

2. What month does school start? _____

3. What is your favorite day of the week? _____

WRITE ON!

On a separate sheet of paper, write about your favorite holiday. What month is it in? Why do you like the holiday? Check to make sure that all of the proper nouns begin with a capital letter.

Name _____ Date _____

Capitalization

- Use a **capital letter** when writing the first letter of a country, nationality, and specific language.
  Example: I learned to speak Spanish for my trip to Mexico.
- Use a **capital letter** when writing the first letter of a sports team, political and civic organization, and national group.
  Example: The Lakers will play at the stadium.

PRACTICE

Use complete sentences to answer the following questions.

1. What languages do you speak? _____
2. What country have you visited or would like to visit? _____
3. What is your favorite professional sports team? _____

Rewrite each sentence using correct capital letters.

1. My favorite football team, the exeter crawdads, is playing at the lemon bowl.

   _____

2. The democratic convention is being held next week.

   _____

3. My sisters and I are members of the girl scouts.

   _____

4. I love the music that is played at padre games.

   _____

5. Do you know how to speak mandarin or cantonese?

   _____

6. My dad has been to germany, france, and england.

   _____

7. green peace is an organization that works to protect our environment.

   _____

8. Tiny Foxtail is a native american.

   _____

WRITE ON!

On a separate sheet of paper, write about someone you know who speaks a different language. In what country is this language primarily spoken? Was it difficult for him or her to learn English? Remember to write the title using capital letters correctly.

Name _____   Date _____

Capitalization

- Use a **capital letter** when writing the first letter of a period and an event, but not a century.

    Example: During the Middle Ages, many changes took place.

- Use a **capital letter** when writing the first letter of a trademark.

    Example: Kleenex® is a brand name for a type of facial tissue.

- Use **capital letters** when writing the abbreviations of specific names.

    Example: When my brother grows up, he wants to work at NASA.

Complete the chart. Make sure to use correct capital letters.

Period or Event	Trademark Names	Abbreviations of Specific Names
Example: Civil War	Example: Styrofoam ™	Example: U.N.
1.	1.	1.
2.	2.	2.
3.	3.	3.
4.	4.	4.

Read the paragraph. Underline the words that should be capitalized.

Joe is a secret shopper. His job is to go into stores and see what kind of customer service or help is provided. His first stop of the day was B & B Importers. Once in the store, he was quickly waited on by j.j., a sales associate. He was shown several copies of rugs from the renaissance as well as original rugs from the ottoman empire. Joe was offered a cup of starbucks® coffee and cream from the local dairy. Joe mentioned he was looking for the items from the commercial shown on TV. j.j. took him right to the items.   Joe gave the sales associate high marks for customer service and filed his report with his company.

Write the words that should have been capitalized correctly on the lines.

_____, _____, _____, _____, _____

Think of a favorite product or era. On a separate sheet of paper, tell what makes the item or time period so great. Remember to use correct capital letters.

Name _____ Date _____

Abbreviated Words

Some of the words we use today have been shortened from longer words. In some cases, the **abbreviated word** takes the place of the longer word.

  Example: Joann, you have a phone call.

  Phone is a shortened form of *telephone.*

PRACTICE

Underline the word in each sentence that is now abbreviated. Write the abbreviated form on the line.

  Example: I will send you a <u>facsimile</u> of the contract.   _____fax_____

1. Jesse's favorite disport is dodgeball.   _____

2. My favorite subject is mathematics.   _____

3. We drove our caravan to the national park.   _____

4. Maxine wore a new pair of pantaloons to school.   _____

5. Theo is such a baseball fanatic!   _____

6. I wish that autobus would be on time for once!   _____

7. Justin is taking pianoforte lessons from Mrs. Gregson.   _____

8. There was an advertisement in the newspaper.   _____

9. Have you ever been to the zoological gardens?   _____

10. Doctors forecast many cases of influenza this winter.   _____

11. Our physics teacher gave us an examination today.   _____

12. "Hand me the microphone," said Vivian.   _____

13. Violet will meet Wilma at three of the clock.   _____

14. We went to see *Batman* at the local cinematograph.   _____

15. The coach said to meet in the gymnasium for practice.   _____

16. For Halloween, I disguised my hair under a periwig.   _____

WRITE ON!

Why do you think these words became abbreviated? Write your response on a separate sheet of paper. Then, share your explanation with a classmate.

Portmanteau Words

A **portmanteau word** is another kind of abbreviated word. In this case, two or more words are put together to create an entirely new word.

Example: *Taximeter cabriolet* is now *taxi* or *cab*.

Write the portmanteau word on the line.

1. breakfast + lunch _____

2. cheese + hamburger _____

3. motor + pedal _____

4. parachute + troops _____

5. smoke + fog _____

6. television + marathon_____

7. twist + whirl_____

8. travel + monologue _____

9. gleam + shimmer _____

10. motor + hotel_____

11. motorcycle + cross country_____

12. splash + spatter _____

13. pix + element_____

14. flame + glare _____

15. flutter + hurry _____

16. clap + crash _____

17. slop + slush _____

18. binary + digit_____

Read each sentence and underline the portmanteau word. Write the meaning of the word on the line.

Example: Today, many teenagers suffer from <u>affluenza</u>.   ____"illness" of having too much____

1. The fraternity threw a fantastic bash.   _____

2. The latest hit film is from Bollywood.   _____

3. Many science fiction films have cyborg characters.   _____

4. In many cafeterias, students use sporks to each lunch. _____

5. The reporter was dumbfounded by the response.   _____

On a separate sheet of paper, make a list of other portmanteau words and the words that were combined to make them. Share your list with a classmate.

Name _____ Date _____

Spelling Rules

Spelling rules serve as a guide for spelling many words in the English language.

Spelling Rule: *I* before *E*

- Use *i before e* when the syllable makes a long *e* sound.
  Example: niece

- Use *e before i* when following the letter *c*.
  Example: receive

- Use *e before i* when the syllable makes a long *a* sound.
  Example: neighbor

Read each sentence. Circle the misspelled word, and write it correctly on the line. (*Note:* Not all sentences will have a misspelled word.)

1. "Good greif, Charlie Brown!" is a famous line from the *Peanuts* comic strip. _____

2. Do not shriek if you see a ghost. _____

3. The class recieved a package from their overseas pen pals. _____

4. The Rumbling Rebels are feirce competitors. _____

5. When did you peirce your ears? _____

6. Make sure to turn in all reciepts to the treasurer. _____

7. The horse always nieghs when he sees us holding carrots. _____

8. The thief got caught when he tried to break into the local jail. _____

9. Try not to decieve people. _____

10. How did handprints get on the cieling? _____

11. The frieght train always rumbles by during the baby's naptime. _____

12. Did you beleive that story? _____

On a separate sheet of paper, write a rhyme to help you remember the three spelling rules. Share your rhyme with the class.

Name _____ Date _____

Spelling Rules

Spelling rules serve as a guide for spelling many words in the English language.

Spelling Rule: Soft *C* and Soft *G*

- When *c* or *g* is followed by *e, i,* or *y*, the sounds are soft.
  Examples: cent, giant, cynic

- To keep a soft *c* or a soft *g* at the end of the word, it must be followed by an *e*.
  Examples: bounce, bounceable, outrageous

- *G* is oftentimes followed by a *u* in order to keep the hard *g* sound.
  Examples: guest, gust, guy

- When *c* or *g* is followed by *a* or *o*, the sounds are hard.
  Examples: cabin, go

PRACTICE

Write the word that answers each clue. Make sure the spelling rules are followed. (*Note:* Some of the words will have the soft *c* and *g* sounds, and others will have the hard *c* and *g* sounds.)

1. A type of tree that smells good (The wood is used to line chests and closets.) _____

2. Besides Fahrenheit, this is another way to measure temperature. _____

3. We had this type of war between the states. _____

4. A stringed instrument _____

5. A meat-eater _____

6. A type of pet (similar to a hamster) _____

7. Another name for a visitor _____

8. Not a dog _____

9. If you are not sure of the answer, you might make one of these. _____

10. Another name for disguise (Detectives or spies might wear one.) _____

11. You are given coins, bills, and *this* after paying for an item. _____

12. Ghandi and Martin Luther King, Jr. fought for this. _____

13. A small, freshwater fish _____

14. You have to pay to travel in this yellow car. _____

WRITE ON!

Explain the rules in a paragraph on a separate sheet of paper. Share your explanation with a classmate.

Name _____ Date _____

Spelling Rules

Spelling rules serve as a guide for spelling many words in the English language.

Spelling Rule: The /k/ Sound at the End of a Word

- Use *ck* after a short vowel in a one-syllable word.
  Examples: tack, brick

- Use *c* after the short vowel at the end of a multi-syllable word.
  Examples: magic, comic

- Use *k* with a consonant, a double vowel, or consonant blend.
  Examples: silk, look, chalk

PRACTICE

Complete each sentence using words that end in the /k/ sound.

1. In case of an earthquake, remember to _____ and cover.

2. We can _____ up on my friend and yell, "Boo!"

3. The earthquake _____ the buildings and homes.

4. Put the dirty dishes in the _____ .

5. A little acorn grows up to be a mighty _____ .

6. Let's go on a _____ at the park.

7. Another name for math is _____ .

8. A _____ keeps track of the time.

9. Remember to _____ before entering someone else's house.

10. Did you _____ your friend for the gift?

11. My sister and I have _____ beds.

12. People _____ their eyes many times each day.

13. Many kinds of exercise clothes have _____ in the waist.

14. Did you _____ your bag for the trip?

15. What kind of _____ do you like to listen to?

16. When I had strep throat, the doctor gave me some _____ .

WRITE ON!

On a separate sheet of paper, sort all of the words used to complete the sentences by how the /k/ sound is spelled. Do they follow the spelling rules?

Name _____   Date _____

Spelling Rules

Spelling rules serve as a guide for spelling many words in the English language.

Spelling Rule: Words Beginning with *C* or *K*

- Use a *c* if it is followed by an *a, o,* or *u.*
  Examples: camp, cot, cub

- Use a *k* if it is followed by an *e* or an *i.*
  Examples: kept, kitchen

PRACTICE

Write the word that answers each clue. Make sure the spelling rules are followed.

1. A prickly desert plant   _____

2. What you eat on your birthday   _____

3. It keeps track of the months.   _____

4. A type of skirt worn by Scottish men   _____

5. A baby cow   _____

6. Sacramento is this state's capital.   _____

7. A type of toy flown in the air   _____

8. Not straight hair   _____

9. You drink from this.   _____

10. To hit a ball with one's foot   _____

11. A country north of the United States   _____

12. The room where food is prepared   _____

13. Use this to open a lock   _____

14. A hard, brown fruit that grows in trees   _____

15. Not mustard   _____

16. Not the queen   _____

WRITE ON!

On a separate sheet of paper, write four statements that describe an item that begins with a *c* or a *k.*
Exchange papers with a classmate. Ask the classmate to write the word for each statement.

Name _____   Date _____

Spelling Rules

Spelling rules serve as a guide for spelling many words in the English language.

Spelling Rule: *Ch* and *Tch*

- If the /ch/ sound follows a short vowel, use *tch*.

  Examples: patch, fetch, hopscotch

- If the /ch/ sound follows a long vowel or a consonant, use *ch*.

  Examples: peach, bunch

Complete each sentence with the correct word.

1. When will they _____ the rocket?

2. You can buy many types of meat at the _____ shop.

3. Some dogs enjoy playing _____ .

4. Each day the professors _____ us a new spelling rule.

5. If you get lost in the woods, we will send out a _____ party for you.

6. Simon lost control of the car, and it went into the _____ .

7. Tomatoes are used to make _____ .

8. The _____ throws a terrific curve ball.

9. On St. Patrick's day, people will be _____ if they are not wearing green.

10. When my dog has an _____ , he rolls on his back to rub it.

11. Could you _____ my back?

12. I need a _____ to light the fire.

13. An artist will make a rough _____ before making the actual drawing.

14. Let's meet at the green park _____ .

Write three more words that fit each spelling rule.

1. Words with *tch*: _____ , _____ , _____

2. Words with *ch*: _____ , _____ , _____

WRITE ON!

On a separate sheet of paper, write about a topic of your choice. Include words that fit the spelling rules.

Name _____   Date _____

Acronyms

An **acronym** is an abbreviation pronounced as a word. An acronym is spelled with all capital letters. There are no periods between the letters.

Example: Absent Without Leave   AWOL

PRACTICE

Write the acronym for each item.

1. Beginner's All-purpose Symbolic Instruction Code   _____

2. Radio Detecting and Ranging   _____

3. North Atlantic Treaty Organization   _____

4. Reading is Fundamental   _____

5. National Organization for Women   _____

6. Fabbrica Italiana Automobili Torino   _____

7. Read-Only Memory   _____

8. Light Amplification by Stimulated Emission of Radiation   _____

9. Zone Improvement Plan   _____

10. Group Against Smog and Pollution   _____

11. Sound Navigation and Ranging   _____

12. As Soon as Possible   _____

13. False Evidence Appearing Real   _____

14. Hazardous Material   _____

15. Personal Identification Number   _____

16. To Insure Prompt Service   _____

17. Special Weapons Action Team   _____

18. Distant Early Warning Line   _____

19. Together Everyone Achieves More   _____

20. National Aeronautics and Space Administration   _____

WRITE ON!

On a separate sheet of paper, create four of your own acronyms. Share them with a classmate.

Name _____   Date _____

Words Known by Their Initials

Some words or phrases are commonly referred to only by their initials. Each initial is read one at a time. Each initial is capitalized.

Example: Rest in Peace   RIP

Write the initials for each word or phrase.

1. Very Important Person _____

2. Recreational Vehicle _____

3. Unidentified Flying Object _____

4. Revolutions Per Minute _____

5. Certified Public Accountant _____

6. Martin Luther King, Jr. _____

7. Private Investigator _____

8. New in the Box _____

9. Tender Loving Care _____

10. Thank Goodness It's Friday _____

11. Extra Terrestrial _____

12. Public Address _____

13. For Your Information _____

14. Identification _____

15. Also Known As _____

16. Mind Your Own Business _____

17. Post Script _____

18. Bacon, Lettuce, and Tomato _____

19. Air Conditioning _____

20. Intelligence Quotient _____

On a separate sheet of paper, write four sentences. Use a set of initials in each sentence.

Name _____   Date _____

Proofreading

Proofreading means checking a piece of writing for errors.

Use the following proofreading marks to edit (correct) each sentence:

| . = period | , = comma | ' = apostrophe | **a** = capital letter |
| **^** = caret/insert a word | **so** = spell out | | **sp** = spelling/spelling error |

1. jeannine and tim were driving home from the store.

2. Put the glass of water on top of the table

3. Have you seen where dad put my notebook?

4. The report cards our handed out on friday.

5. In Jan., we will start a new semester at school.

6. A truck skidded flipped over and spilled all of its contents all over the highway.

7. Dont bother the bears at the zoo and don't make fun of the monkeys, either.

8. Have you seen dora?

9. When i get home from work I take off my shoes and relax in the chair.

10. When it snows, snowplows from david's snow shop clear the streets.

11. I live at 232 W. Park Place Chicago Illinois.

12. To get to the park, go n. on First St. and turn e. on Pine Blvd.

On a separate sheet of paper, write four sentences with errors in punctuation and/or spelling. Exchange papers with a classmate. Ask the classmate to proofread the paper. Did the classmate find all of the errors?

Name _____   Date _____

Proofreading

Proofreading means checking a piece of writing for errors.

Use the following proofreading marks to edit (correct) the letter below:

. = period   **,** = comma   **'** = apostrophe   **a̲** = capital letter
^ = caret/insert a word   **so** = spell out   **sp** = spelling/spelling error

---

June 22 2009

To whom it may concern:

I am writing to you about one of your products. i recently purchased one of your pens, the Super gel Writer. I thunk the Super Gel Writer is one of the best pens on the market. It write so smoothly and the ink doesnt smudge. This is so important because I am left-handed. With some pens, the ink dries so slow that us lefties end up smearing it all over the paper when we write. And we lefties are then stuck walking around with ink stains on hands or, even worse, on clothes! Thank u for this grate product!

You're faithful customer,

I. M. Writer

Have you ever bought a product that you thought was fantastic? Or, have you ever bought a product that was terrible? On a separate sheet of paper, write a letter to the company telling what was so great (or so awful) about the product. Share your letter with the class.

ANSWER KEY

Warm-Up 1 (page 8)
1. first person   2. third person   3. second person

Warm-Up 2 (page 9)
1. it	6. we	1. He/She	6. he
2. it	7. it	2. He/She	7. He
3. it	8. he	3. They	8. They
4. they	9. I	4. She	9. He/She
5. she	10. they	5. He	10. They

Warm-Up 3 (page 10)
1. Mrs. Greenstone/she
2. Rover/It
3. Stella, Jim, and I/We
4. Dean and Stacy/They
5. Mom and Dad/They
6. Recycle-R-Us and Eco-Green/They
7. Homework/It
8. Ken/He
9. Trees/They
10. Parents/They
11. Doug/He
12. Grace, Bea, and Maggie/They

Check to make sure the student has written sentences using the subject pronouns indicated.

Warm-Up 4 (page 11)
When the hamburger was brought to **him**, he took a big bite of the juicy burger.
Ralph turned to **us** and said, "Wow! This is the best burger ever!"
When it was brought to **us**, we told **them**, "Thanks! We can't wait to eat it all!"
So, the waiter brought Sue a doggie bag to take **it** home.
Ralph, Sue, and I left **them** a big tip.

Warm-Up 5 (page 12)
1. That is their house. *or* That house is theirs.
2. Our school is over a hundred years old. *or* Ours is over a hundred years old.
3. Her collage is full of photographs and cards. *or* Hers is full of photographs and cards.
4. It is his television. *or* That television is his.
5. This is his/her laptop. *or* This laptop is his/hers.

Warm-Up 6 (page 13)
1. Underline <u>Fred, Willard, Jim,</u> and <u>his</u>; no agreement in number
2. Underline <u>you</u> and <u>she</u>; no agreement in person
3. Underline <u>Raphael, Roberta,</u> and <u>we</u>; no agreement in person
4. Underline <u>Keith</u> and <u>she</u>; no agreement in gender
5. Underline <u>Enid</u> and <u>they</u>; no agreement in number

Warm-Up 7 (page 14)
Check to make sure the student has used some of the indefinite pronouns in sentences.
Everybody (are) going to the assembly on Friday.
Nobody (are) stamping feet on the floor or banging fists on the tables.
Does anyone (has) any questions?

Warm-Up 8 (page 15)
1. Nobody/No one/Somebody/Someone
2. anything/something
3. Both/A few/Many/Others/Several/All/Most/None/Some
4. Both/A few/Many/Several/All/More/Most/Some
5. Neither/One
6. Both/A few/Many/Several/All/Most/Some
7. Another/Each/Either/Every/Neither/One
8. Both/A few/Many/Several/More/Most/Some

Warm-Up 9 (page 16)
Check to make sure the student has written each sentence with a subject pronoun and an intensive pronoun.
I, <u>myself</u>, actually built a miniature log cabin using pretzels.
Mr. Rogers, <u>himself</u>, was so impressed with my pretzel log cabin that he said it should be put in the Smithsonian Museum!
And, I have to admit, I, <u>myself</u>, was proud of me, too!

I actually built a miniature log cabin using pretzels.
Mr. Rogers was so impressed with my pretzel log cabin that he said it should be put in the Smithsonian Museum!
And, I have to admit, I was proud of me, too!

Warm-Up 10 (page 17)
Check to make sure the student has written each sentence with a subject pronoun and a reflexive pronoun.
He painted all of the booth signs <u>himself</u>.
They outdid <u>themselves</u> this year.
I was very proud of <u>myself</u>.

Warm-Up 11 (page 18)
1. This tastes awful!
2. These are for you.
3. These are fantastic!
4. That is an incredible invention.
5. Those belonged to my grandmother.

Warm-Up 12 (page 19)
1. who	3. whomever	5. who	7. whom	9. whom
2. whoever	4. whom	6. whom	8. who	10. whom

Warm-Up 13 (page 20)
1. that	3. that	5. whatever
2. which	4. which	6. that

Check to make sure the student has written each sentence with a relative pronoun.

Warm-Up 14 (page 21)
1. Whose lunch money is this?
2. Who will take the chocolate cupcake with sprinkles on top? *or* What cupcake do you want?
3. Who was knocking at the door?
4. Whom was the package for? *or* For whom was the package?
5. What did Professor Geary want to know?
6. Who has been to Seattle, Washington, many times?
7. Whose bike is blocking the driveway?
8. What will we have for dinner tonight?
9. Which uniforms does the coach like best? *or* Who likes the blue and silver uniforms best?
10. Whom is the gift for? *or* What occasion is the gift for?

Warm-Up 15 (page 22)
1. The seamstress' thread colors are different and bright.
2. The sailor's hat flew overboard.
3. The witness' testimony rang true.
4. Eli's older brother is in eighth grade.
5. The class' project was to write reports on insects.

ANSWER KEY

Warm-Up 16 (page 23)
1. Kris' marbles fell down onto the classroom floor.
2. Mr. Veen's paperwork is important.
3. The principals' meeting was held in the school library.
4. The lockers' doors were in need of repair.
5. Lucas' signs were made by his parents.

Warm-Up 17 (page 24)
1. Bill and Will's room is always spotless.
2. The geese's feathers flew all around the sky before dropping to the ground.
3. The mice's homes were made in the walls of the house.
4. The ceiling and door's paint was cracked and peeling.
5. The pot and pan's handles were made of walnut.
6. The people's votes were counted by hand.

Warm-Up 18 (page 25)
1. Sean's and Deandre's injuries kept the team from winning the championship.
2. The chairman of the board's declaration settled the argument.
3. Rosa's and Gabe's scores were the best and the worst in the class.
4. My brother-in-law's business is doing well.
5. Teddy's and Franklin's inventions have helped people from many different generations.

Warm-Up 19 (page 26)
1. feet 3. dice 5. oxen
2. mice 4. women 6. teeth

1. mans/men 2. womans/women 3. children/child

My family and I were playing a game called "Catch an ~~Oxen~~." [Ox]
My brother was a ~~mice~~. [mouse]

On the first roll of the dice, I moved ahead three spaces and landed in the space that said, "Lost a ~~teeth~~, move back two [tooth] spaces."

He landed in the space that said, "Fell out of a tree and broke your leg in ~~halves~~. Go back to Start." [half]

Warm-Up 20 (page 27)
1. plural 3. singular 5. plural 7. plural
2. singular 4. plural 6. singular 8. plural
Check to make sure the student has answered each question.
Possible answers include:
The noun is singular if the word "a" is before the noun or if a singular verb is used.
The noun is plural if a number word (larger than one) is before the noun or if the plural form of a verb is used.

Warm-Up 21 (page 28)
1. quail/quails 5. shrimp/shrimps
2. grouse/grouse 6. fish/fishes
3. flounder/flounders 7. herring/herrings
4. salmon/salmons 8. trout/trout

One morning, we saw the tracks from elk! We could tell by the different sizes of the tracks that the elk might have been a family.
We watched the different fish swim about in the cool water.
We must have seen twenty ~~trouts~~! On our return to the cabin, we heard the morning call of the quail, and we knew it was time for breakfast.

Warm-Up 22 (page 29)
1. is/was 5. is/was 8. are/were
2. are/were 6. are/were 9. has
3. are/were 7. is/was 10. are/were
4. is/was
Check to make sure the student has written four collective nouns and four sentences that contain those collective nouns.

Warm-Up 23 (page 30)
Check to make sure the student has written each sentence with a helping verb.
Yesterday, my dog, Dagney, was acting strangely. She had been gathering old towels and blankets and dragging them to a corner.
When I checked on Dagney later, you wouldn't believe what I saw. Dagney had had three puppies! Dagney was a mom!

Warm-Up 24 (page 31)
Mr. Mitchell is always running behind schedule. He says that it is because he has too many things to do. One day, he said that he might be late because his cat was stuck in a tree, and he could not wake his dog up! His wife, Mrs. Mitchell, has even tried setting the clocks ahead by ten minutes. She did this in hopes that it would help her husband get to his appointments on time. It worked for a while, until the power went out, and Mr. Mitchell had to reset all of the clocks!
Check to make sure the student has written suggestions.
Check to make sure the student has used each helping verb in a sentence.

Warm-Up 25 (page 32)
Check to make sure the student has written eight regular verbs in the present and past tense.
Once a load of clothes is ~~washes~~ in the washer, the load is [washed] ~~moving~~ to the dryer. [moved]
Once the clothes are dry, they are ~~folden~~ and placed into bins. [folded]

Warm-Up 26 (page 33)
1. drank 6. paid 11. wrote 16. drew
2. kept 7. ran 12. won 17. saw
3. hung 8. said 13. slept 18. fed
4. gave 9. stung 14. sat 19. left
5. made 10. wore 15. thought 20. lied/laid

Shawn ~~run~~ all the way home. [ran]
He ~~thinked~~ his parents would be excited for him, but he [thought] ~~knowed~~ his sister would think he ~~maked~~ it all up. [knew] [made]

They would say things like, "We are so proud of you," and "You ~~outdoed~~ yourself!" Shawn ~~feeled~~ like he had ~~winned~~ [outdid] [felt] [won] the lottery!

Warm-Up 27 (page 34)
1. future tense 2. present tense 3. past tense
Paragraph #1: future tense
Paragraph #2: past tense
Paragraph #3: present tense

ANSWER KEY

Warm-Up 28 (page 35)

Verb	Present Tense	Past Tense	Future Tense
Example: become	become	became	become
1. bring	bring	brought	bring
2. grow	grow	grew	grow
3. come	come	came	come
4. freeze	freeze	froze	freeze
5. do	do	did	do
6. leave	leave	left	leave
7. go	go	went	go
8. keep	keep	kept	keep
9. arise	arise	arose	arise
10. buy	buy	bought	buy
11. fly	fly	flew	fly
12. know	know	knew	know
13. pay	pay	paid	pay
14. break	break	broke	break
15. teach	teach	taught	teach
16. hit	hit	hit	hit
17. ride	ride	rode	ride
18. take	take	took	take

Warm-Up 29 (page 36)
1. future perfect tense
2. past perfect tense
3. past perfect tense
4. present perfect tense
5. future perfect tense
6. present perfect tense
Check to make sure the student has written a sentence to illustrate each verb tense.

Warm-Up 30 (page 37)
Check to make sure the student has written an adjective for each word.
Check to make sure the student has written four adjectives to describe a bird.
Check to make sure the student has written a paragraph about the bird using each adjective.

Warm-Up 31 (page 38)
Check to make sure the student has completed each sentence with an adjective.

Warm-Up 32 (page 39)
1. The thin, decomposing lighthouse has guided ships and sailors for many years.
2. The short, redheaded child wants a balloon.
3. The old, leather couch was bought for the new house.
4. My grandma wore a long, loud muumuu to the party.
5. The coldhearted, hardheaded miser refused to give a penny to the orphan.
6. The fire department raced to rescue the fat, fluffy feline stuck in a tree.

Warm-Up 33 (page 40)
1. more/less vibrant
2. more/less confused
3. more/less clever
4. stronger
5. crazier
6. more/less comfortable
7. prettier
8. flashier
9. more/less popular
10. more/less alike
11. healthier
12. more/less trivial

Warm-Up 34 (page 41)
1. craziest
2. luckiest
3. most/least colorful
4. most/least interesting
5. most/least gracious
6. most/least efficient
7. most/least trouble
8. loudest
9. most/least urgent
10. most/least delicious
11. brightest
12. freshest

Warm-Up 35 (page 42)
Check to make sure the student has used each adjective as a comparative or superlative adjective in a sentence.

Over a hundred years ago, the ~~most~~ cleverest people made this bridge. The bridge is of the most ~~simpler~~ simple design, just wood and rope. The bridge spans the most ~~narrowest~~ narrow part of the Giganto River. Most of the time, the moving water makes the ~~more~~ quietest of sounds. During heavy rain, the moving water becomes less ~~pleasanter~~ pleasant.

Warm-Up 36 (page 43)

Adjective	Comparative (two items)	Superlative (three or more items)
good	better	best
bad	worse	worst
far	farther	farthest
little	less	least
many	more	most

1. little, less, least
2. many, more, most
3. bad, worse, worst
4. good, better, best

Warm-Up 37 (page 44)
1. bad   2. badly   3. bad   4. badly   5. bad   6. bad   7. bad   8. badly   9. bad   10. badly

Warm-Up 38 (page 45)
1. good   2. well   3. good/well   4. good   5. well   6. good   7. well   8. good   9. good   10. well   11. well   12. good   13. good   14. well

Warm-Up 39 (page 46)
Sally and Charlotte were **really** good friends.
They usually met at Sally's house because her craft room was **really** neat and tidy. Charlotte kept her craft supplies in the **really** tall closet. Charlotte carefully opened her box and picked out some **really** tiny beads. Charlotte was **really** good at beading.
People said that she had a **real** talent for beading.
Sally had **real** flowers drying in a box and plastic flowers in a different box.
She could even make plastic flowers look **real**.
Check to make sure the student has written each sentence correctly using the words *real* and *really*.

Warm-Up 40 (page 47)
Check to make sure the student has used an adverb in each sentence and has written what question it answers.

Warm-Up 41 (page 48)
1. lightly
2. nicely
3. quickly
4. terribly
5. patiently
6. slowly
7. First
8. gently
9. next
10. delightfully
11. Soon, playfully
12. gracefully
13. sincerely
14. noisily
Check to make sure the student has written an adverb for each event.

ANSWER KEY

Warm-Up 42 (page 49)

Manner	Place	Frequency	Time	Purpose
1. easily	1. abroad	1. often	1. after	1. because
2. fast	2. here	2. rarely	2. before	2. in order to
3. patiently	3. outside	3. seldom	3. next	3. since
4. quietly	4. somewhere	4. usually	4. now	4. so that

Check to make sure the student has used an adverb from above in each sentence.

Warm-Up 43 (page 50)
Check to make sure the student has written four adverbs and has used them in comparative and superlative sentences.

Warm-Up 44 (page 51)
Check to make sure the student has completed each sentence with an adverb or an adverbial phrase that answers the question.

Warm-Up 45 (page 52)
Check to make sure the student has circled all of the words.
1. next to/in front of/on top of/under/near
2. next to/in front of/over/under/near
3. in front of/among/near
4. out of
5. before/next to/in front of/among/near
6. on top of/next to/under/near/on the back of
7. next to/in front of/near
8. next to/in front of/at/near
9. on top of/next to/in front of/under/among/near
10. next to/across/near

Each day after school, Samantha throws her backpack <u>on</u> her bed. She pulls her headphones <u>out from under</u> her pillow and listens to music <u>on</u> her radio. When she is done, she puts the headphones and radio <u>on top of</u> her dresser. Samantha opens her backpack and takes <u>out</u> her binder. <u>In the front of</u> the binder is her agenda.
She finds paper <u>inside</u> her desk drawer and gets to work.

Warm-Up 46 (page 53)
Check to make sure the student has answered each question and has circled the preposition or prepositional phrase that indicates location in the answer.

Warm-Up 47 (page 54)
Check to make sure the student has circled the following sentences:
2. After watching the news, Dad went to sleep.
3. Between innings, the crowd stood up and stretched.
4. Inga hasn't missed a day of school since kindergarten.
6. Within the hour, we will have a fire drill.
8. Until now, David had never had a cavity.
10. From now on, nobody should be late to practice.
11. During a moment of silence, Thomas sneezed loudly.

Warm-Up 48 (page 55)
1. after
2. Before
3. At
4. Throughout
5. Between
6. upon
7. Over
8. within
9. Next
10. until
11. Until
12. Near
Check to make sure the student has used a preposition to indicate location in time in each sentence.

Warm-Up 49 (page 56)
1. and
2. nor
3. so
4. or
5. but
6. for
7. yet
Check to make sure the student has used each conjunction in a sentence.

Warm-Up 50 (page 57)
1. either/or
2. both/and, neither/nor, not only/but also
3. as/as
4. both/and, neither/nor
5. both/and, neither/nor
6. either/or
7. either/or
8. both/and, neither/nor, not only/but also
9. not only/but also, both/and, neither/nor, either/or
10. both/and, neither/nor, not only/but also
11. whether/or
12. whether/or

Warm-Up 51 (page 58)
1. after/even though/now that/once
2. After/As long as/Because/Now that/Once/Since/When/Whenever
3. as if/as though
4. After/If/Now that/Once/When/Whenever
5. Before/Until
6. unless
7. Until
8. Because/Now that/Since/While
9. After/When/Whenever/Wherever
10. before/if/when
Check to make sure the student has written each sentence using a subordinating conjunction.

Warm-Up 52 (page 59)
1. than
2. Then
3. then
4. then
5. then
6. then
7. then
8. than
9. than
10. then
11. then
12. than
13. than
14. then

Warm-Up 53 (page 60)
1. like
2. such
3. such
4. as
5. As
6. like
7. like
8. such
Check to make sure the student has written each sentence with *like, as,* and *such.*

Warm-Up 54 (page 61)
1. Ouch
2. Whoa
3. Aha
4. Yikes
5. Eeek
6. Ugggh
7. Wait
8. Phew
9. Sweet
10. Ooops
11. Well
12. Yes
13. Uh oh
14. Oh
15. No
16. Help
17. Ahhhhhh
18. Wow
Check to make sure the student has listed four other interjections.

ANSWER KEY

Warm-Up 55 (page 62)
1. declarative
2. imperative
3. exclamatory
4. interrogative

The Golden Gate Bridge is in San Francisco, California. Do you know when the bridge was finished? It was finished in 1937. It took four years to build, and they actually finished it under budget! At the time, it was the longest suspension bridge in the world! The bridge is painted a color called international orange. The architect of the bridge thought that this color was more appropriate than gray or black.

Warm-Up 56 (page 63)
1. The train stopped.
2. The door shut.
3. The doctor did rounds.
4. Mrs. Brown is a kind person.
5. The lights flickered.

The movie crew started filming.
The stunt double jumped.
He landed gently onto a giant airbag.
He wanted to rest.
Check to make sure the student has written three simple sentences.

Warm-Up 57 (page 64)
1. Tracy worked on the car, and she built a tree house.
2. Vic watched the latest action movie, and he ate a huge tub of popcorn.
3. Bonnie and Len wanted to do something fun, so they made a house out of playing cards.
4. Tina's alarm clock did not go off, so she missed the bus.
5. Nick thought he was a shoe-in for the job, but/yet he botched the entire interview.
6. Kim completed her homework, but Rover ate the assignments.
7. The chef prepared dinner, and the baker made the dessert.
8. The singer went on tour, but/yet her family stayed home.

Check to make sure the student has written two compound sentences and has circled the coordinating conjunctions.

Warm-Up 58 (page 65)
Sample answers:
1. Because she is paid well, Beth babysits the neighborhood children.
2. Even though it was a school night, Mom said that I could stay up late.
3. Before it was closing time, the bakery had two fruit pies left.
4. Since we were at the beach, we made a sandcastle.
5. After we eat dinner, my family enjoys playing board games.

Warm-Up 59 (page 66)
Paragraph #1
Although I studied hard, I did not pass the test, and I will have to retake the class.

Because I don't know how to swim, my aunt had signed me up for swim lessons, and she had inquired about a course in water safety.

Paragraph #2
Because he didn't want the hens to peck at his hand, he would be fast, but he would also be gentle.

When he finished his chores, it was time for breakfast, and then it was off to the bus stop to catch the bus.

Check to make sure the student has written three compound-complex sentences.

Warm-Up 60 (page 67)
1. SS	3. CS	5. SS	7. CX	9. CS	11. XS
2. XS	4. CX	6. SS	8. CS	10. CX	12. XS

Warm-Up 61 (page 68)
Sample answers:
1. to hear   2. napping   3. students   4. bird
1. Greg and Joe watched television, ate pizza, and played football.
2. Amanda woke up, got dressed, and caught the bus.
3. The old house's windows were cracked, dirty, and broken.
4. The bicycle has large wheels, a big seat, and tall handlebars.
5. Make sure you stir the mixture, pour it into the pan, and smooth it out.
6. The peacock's feathers were bright, shiny, and long.

Warm-Up 62 (page 69)
Check to make sure the student has underlined the sentences that do not have parallel structure.

Paragraph #1
To make sure everything went well, Madge read her notes, practiced her speech, and pretended to answer her questions. After being introduced, Madge gave her speech, answered questions, and sat down.

Paragraph #2
They liked the same sports, attended the same schools, and enjoyed the same foods.
On the weekends, their parents would find them at the skate park practicing flips, turns, and jumps.

Paragraph #3
She was in charge of answering phones, writing messages, and greeting patients.
When she had a spare minute, Gracie filed forms, updated charts, and shredded papers.

Warm-Up 63 (page 70)
Check to make sure the student has completed the Transitional Words activity page.

Warm-Up 64 (page 71)
Check to make sure the student has written the steps for doing a task and has underlined the transitional words.

Warm-Up 65 (page 72)
Check to make sure the student has written about a problem and has underlined the transitional words.

Warm-Up 66 (page 73)
Check to make sure the student has written about the day and has underlined the transitional words.

Warm-Up 67 (page 74)
A. 4, 2, 1, 3   B. 4, 1, 3, 2   C. 1, 4, 3, 2

Warm-Up 68 (page 75)
Check to make sure the student has completed the Sequential Order activity page.

ANSWER KEY

Warm-Up 69 (page 76)
1. away
2. one circle/wheel
3. one-hundredth of a meter
4. before the game
5. three colors
6. not honest
7. two muscles
8. wrong spelling
9. not active
10. before school
11. not responsible or not showing care
12. not legal
13. self move
14. not possible
15. wrong fortune
16. one tone
17. finish again
18. one language

Bev and Stu went to the <u>preshow</u> at the local circus. At the <u>preshow</u>, Bev and Stu watched a clown ride a <u>unicycle</u>. He acted like he was going to fall and then <u>regained</u> his balance. Soon, a bear came out riding a <u>bicycle</u>. The bear clapped its paws, and its <u>triplets</u> came tumbling out on the stage. Each bear cub seemed to do the most <u>impossible</u> stunts ever. The first bear cub rode a <u>tricycle</u>. The second bear cub flexed its <u>biceps</u> before high-stepping across the stage. The third bear cub jumped on its mom's shoulders, <u>disembarked</u>, and <u>returned</u> to the center of the stage.

Warm-Up 70 (page 77)
1. to what extent, very often
2. to form bigger
3. state of being kind
4. without a penny
5. full of joy
6. the act of preparing
7. able to be eaten
8. act of being confused
9. study of animals
10. most tall
11. state of comfort
12. to scare
13. without meat
14. one who acts
15. able to be read
16. state of being happy

1. geology
2. beautiful
3. richest
4. likeable
5. headless
6. discussion

Warm-Up 71 (page 78)
Sample answers:
bifold: two folds
return: to go back
impossible: not possible
misdeed: wrong deed
disallow: not allow
tasteless: without taste
baker: one who bakes
gentleness: state of being gentle
joyful: full of joy
likeable: able to be liked

Warm-Up 72 (page 79)
1. dated after
2. not an issue
3. a device used to communicate
4. under standard, not up to par
5. not believing
6. to go over again
7. to qualify before
8. to remove, to take off

Warm-Up 73 (page 80)
1. to hang something that is unprocessed
2. a machine that pulls
3. written on
4. to return
5. to carry from one location to another
6. to drive forward
7. to walk (or move) forward
8. to discard or throw out

Warm-Up 74 (page 81)
1. to pull away
2. to turn back
3. to throw between
4. to write after
5. to say before
6. to write before
7. to walk backward, to go backwards
8. to drive backward
9. to pull under
10. to carry across

Warm-Up 75 (page 82)
1. small view, used to view small things
2. all across
3. a person's own signature
4. new classical
5. life story
6. measuring device of heat
7. life study
8. one circle
9. not common, unusual, not typical
10. all view

The museum was built in a <u>neoclassical</u> style by the well-known artist, Flavia Timmons. As part of her design, <u>microorganisms</u> were engraved on the handrails. Ms. Timmons showed her interest in <u>biology</u> by using living plants as part of the landscape. When we climbed one of the many towers, we had a <u>panoramic</u> view of the museum and its surrounding land. Throughout the landscape, Ms. Timmons had <u>monoliths</u> carved from stone.

Warm-Up 76 (page 83)
1. something that measures time
2. run by the people
3. feeling for others
4. child's doctor
5. a machine that produces sound
6. change form
7. looks and acts like a human
8. organized by time

Warm-Up 77 (page 84)
Sample answers:
anamorph: without form
microphone: small sound
demographic: recording of people

Warm-Up 78 (page 85)
1. long distance sound/speaker
2. resembling a human
3. person who is active
4. long distance writing
5. speech about travel
6. self-signatures, self-writing
7. fears
8. lover of sound

Warm-Up 79 (page 86)
1. a type of dried meat
2. a type of tree
3. coverings for the legs
4. an insect
5. to not allow
6. to pirate the stage, not allow anyone to speak
7. a musical instrument

Warm-Up 80 (page 87)
1. information about a job or sale found in printed material
2. someone who stands up for others
3. to bother

4. to make judgments without information
5. to stop
6. a piece of land going out into the sea
7. a dried square of bread
8. a coin worth ten cents
9. an eating utensil
10. a movement

Warm-Up 81 (page 88)
1. to raise a fuss
2. a knowledgeable person, an expert
3. to talk to someone, to get information
4. to be okay, acceptable
5. a day of rest
6. a sea monster or whale

Warm-Up 82 (page 89)
1. to raise a ruckus, a screaming person
2. wet ground
3. plenty
4. fake
5. many of something
6. tiny pieces

Warm-Up 83 (page 90)
Sample answers:

1. laughed at	8. appropriate	15. permitted
2. pretend	9. faithful	16. consented
3. wrote	10. unique	17. respect
4. dumb	11. repaired	18. job
5. polite	12. disregard	19. commonplace
6. hide	13. considerate	20. against
7. admire	14. know	

1. pretend	4. considerate	7. talk over	9. costume
2. wrote	5. aware	8. soda	10. suitable
3. wrote	6. denied		

Warm-Up 84 (page 91)
Sample answers:
1. dimension, magnitude
2. huge, enormous
3. fluffy, squishy
4. instructor, professor
5. foliage, flower
6. dish, platter

riding=pedaling
stop=brake
parked=stopped
shop=parlor
asked=inquired
said=replied
man behind the counter=storekeeper
said=answered
boys=lads
replied=chorused

Warm-Up 85 (page 92)
Sample answers:

1. accepts	5. bravery	9. light	13. sharp
2. plain	6. true	10. slim	14. extraordinary
3. sick	7. fixed	11. impatient	15. graceful
4. admits	8. yelled	12. fancy	16. entertain

1. messiest	3. never	5. whispers	7. lost
2. least	4. unpleasant	6. lost	8. green

1. awful, terrible
2. terrific, fabulous
3. kind, pleasant

Warm-Up 86 (page 93)
Sample answers:

1. adult	4. dry	7. praise
2. many	5. separate	8. socialite
3. neat	6. outcast	

Paragraph #1
Rebecca was so **disappointed**. She had **lost** a raffle ticket on the ground. She knew that this was the **losing** ticket. The **last** prize was a gift certificate to the local computer store. With the gift certificate, Rebecca was going to buy an **old** digital camera. She kept her fingers crossed and hoped they would call out the raffle ticket's **letters**.

Paragraph #2
Richie was so **thrilled**. His team played their hearts out, but they still **won** the game. What went **right**? Richie replayed the game over and over in his **feet**. Maybe if we had made that **first** basket, the game's outcome might have been different. Maybe if Benny had been on the **court**, we might have stood a chance.

Warm-Up 87 (page 94)

1. antonyms	6. antonyms	11. synonyms
2. synonyms	7. synonyms	12. synonyms
3. antonyms	8. synonyms	13. synonyms
4. synonyms	9. antonyms	14. antonyms
5. synonyms	10. synonyms	

Sample answers:

1. starving, full	5. misplaced, found
2. fearless, scared	6. quick, slow
3. ferocious, friendly	7. herbivore, meat-eater
4. spender, saver	8. attentive, sloppy

Warm-Up 88 (page 95)
Sample answers:

Word	Meaning #1	Meaning #2	Same or Different Pronunciation
Ex. saw	to have seen	a tool used to cut wood	same
1. bass	type of fish	a low voice or instrument	different
2. buffet	all-you-can-eat meal	a serving table	same
3. dove	a type of bird	to have plunged into something	different
4. number	to assign numerals in sequence	how many	same
5. present	at this time	a gift	same
6. record	a vinyl disc that plays music	to preserve in writing	different
7. sewer	where waste goes	a person who sews	different
8. use	to consume	put something into action, to manipulate someone	same
9. wind	to turn a dial	blowing air	different
10. wound	an injury	past tense of wind, to have turned a dial	different

Check to make sure the student has answered the question.

Warm-Up 89 (page 96)
Check to make sure the student has used each homograph two different ways.

Warm-Up 90 (page 97)
1. a, c   2. a, b   3. c   4. a, c

Warm-Up 91 (page 98)
1. b   2. c   3. c   4. b

ANSWER KEY

Warm-Up 92 (page 99)
Sample answers:
1. what one is called, to list
2. to smack something with a bat, a success
3. to buy items, a store that sells items
4. to write using a keyboard, a kind or brand
5. an article or essay, material made from a tree
6. to touch, an animal one takes care of

Warm-Up 93 (page 100)
1. so, sew   4. see, sea   7. some, sum
2. flour, flower   5. tale, tail   8. son, sun
3. band, banned   6. aloud, allowed
Sample answers:
1. to join together using stitches
2. the blossom of a plant
3. a star in the solar system
4. an unspecified number
5. to prohibit or not allow
6. salt water that covers Earth's surface
7. a story
8. said with a speaking voice

Warm-Up 94 (page 101)
Sample answers:
1. Do you eat <u>meat</u>?
2. My favorite color is <u>blue</u>.
3. <u>Would</u> you like to be a Girl Scout?
4. A <u>rose</u> is a sweet-smelling flower.
5. I have <u>two</u> siblings.
6. Put the dog <u>in</u> its crate.
7. Remember to say "<u>Hi</u>" to Grandma.
8. I have a lot of <u>hair</u>.

Warm-Up 95 (page 102)
1. there   5. loupe   9. waste   13. pedal
2. stare   6. shoe   10. sent   14. waive
3. steal   7. bare   11. piece   15. worn
4. tacks   8. too   12. buy   16. hall

Warm-Up 96 (page 103)
1. to give the correct answer
2. finishing touch, something nice
3. to cross in the middle of the street, not at a crosswalk
4. extremely quick passage of time
5. something is always going wrong
6. to have patience
7. money set aside for retirement or emergencies
8. to slap another's hand in joy
9. to tell a secret
10. to learn how to do something

Warm-Up 97 (page 104)
1. beating around the bush
2. to cost an arm and a leg
3. cast-iron stomach
4. backseat driver
5. racing against the clock
6. chew someone out
7. blood is thicker than water
8. back to square one
9. crack someone up
10. break a leg

11. down to the wire
12. cut to the chase

Warm-Up 98 (page 105)
1. drives me up the wall
2. don't count your chickens before they hatch
3. get over it
4. hit the books
5. gave her her walking papers
6. everything but the kitchen sink
7. hit the hay
8. take sides
9. goes the extra mile
10. finger lickin' good
11. dry run
12. fuddy-duddy

Warm-Up 99 (page 106)
Sample answers:
1. easy to do
2. was treated the same way he treated others
3. making someone angrier, making things worse
4. in the same situation, have the same problem
5. gets angry quickly
6. does everything possible
7. took on too much
8. something that doesn't work or perform like it should
9. upset or irritated
10. cup of coffee

Warm-Up 100 (page 107)
Paragraph #1
gotten off on the wrong foot, out of the blue, chew out, saved by the bell

Brad had had a bad day. His day got off to a bad start with his teacher. He went up to ask the teacher a question, and, suddenly, he sneezed all over the teacher. The teacher yelled at Brad. Luckily, the bell rang, and Brad was able to escape to his next class.

Paragraph #2
slap on the wrist, apple in her parents' eyes, a taste of his own medicine, get over it

Francine was so upset! Her brother broke her favorite CD, and he didn't get in trouble. Just because her little brother was her parents' favorite child didn't mean he shouldn't be held accountable. Francine wanted to treat her brother's things the same way. She ran into his room in a rage. She looked around to see what she could break, but all he had were cardboard books and stuffed animals. Francine decided to forget about it and went to watch cartoons with her brother.

Warm-Up 101 (page 108)
1. as strong as an ox
2. rumbled like thunder
3. laughs like a hyena
4. like she just rolled out of bed
5. as white as snow
6. as blind as a bat
7. as cute as a button
8. like you've been through a war
9. like a fish out of water
10. like a fresh mint

11. as busy as a beaver
12. as clean as a whistle
13. like a computer
14. like a hamster in a wheel
15. as happy as a clam
16. as hungry as a bear
17. like a lion
18. like a bird

Check to make sure the student has completed each simile.

Warm-Up 102 (page 109)
Sample answers:
1. like a bull in a china shop (She is clumsy and bumps into things.)
2. runs like the wind (He is a fast runner.)
3. as proud as a peacock (He is filled with pride and it shows.)
4. as bright as a new penny (Her eyes are bright and clear.)
5. like the cat who ate the canary (She has a smug look on her face.)
6. as nimble as a monkey (He is very quick and agile.)
7. eats like a bird (She does not eat very much.)
8. like two weasels in a bag (The fight had a lot of screaming and scrambling.)
9. as clear as mud (The directions were not very clear.)
10. as light as a feather (She doesn't weigh very much.)

Warm-Up 103 (page 110)
Paragraph #1
The building stood tall like a mountain. With the antenna on its top, it looked like a missile getting ready for take off. The windows were as shiny as aluminum foil.

Paragraph #2
The afternoon was as hot as a sauna, but it was as cool as a refrigerator in the shade. Soon, Leo was snoring like a buzz saw as the hammock rocked him like a baby.

Paragraph #3
The tiny mouse peeked from its hole and then ran as quick as a wink across the cat's whiskers.
The mouse gave a squeak as loud as a lion's roar. The mouse used its tail like a whip and snapped it across the cat's nose. The cat's nose felt as burned as lit firewood.

Paragraph #4
It looked like steam was coming from his ears. He stomped his feet like a bull getting ready to charge. He rolled his hands into fists as big as boulders and shook them into the air. He was as angry as a rattlesnake.

Warm-Up 104 (page 111)
Sample answers:
1. It is extremely hot and steamy.
2. She knows a lot of information.
3. The dog is very heavy.
4. The leaves were being blown around.
5. She has a lot of good luck.
6. She hit the wrong keys.
7. Her smile was big and showed a lot of teeth.
8. His feet smelled extremely bad.
9. He doesn't listen to reason.
10. She had a lot of ideas.

Warm-Up 105 (page 112)
Sample answers:
1. It's raining really hard.
2. Around here, life slows down.
3. Jenna is very special to her dad.
4. She wasn't born yet.
5. He has a lot of money.
6. Mom is exhausted.
7. She spoiled the party.
8. He eats a lot.
9. She is not a graceful dancer.
10. Kevin was furious.

Warm-Up 106 (page 113)
Paragraph #1
The baby was positively sunny!
When she tried to remove the baby's pacifier, she found it cemented in the baby's mouth.

Paragraph #2
The football player leapt with a ballerina's grace into the air to catch the football. He landed softer than a cloud on one foot and thundered down the field to score the winning touchdown.

Paragraph #3
Babe found the homework to be a breeze. She blasted through the math assignment and then glided through the spelling.
She stirred the mixture in a frenzy of anticipation. At her first bite, Babe thought she tasted a bit of heaven.

Warm-Up 107 (page 114)
Check to make sure the student has written three metaphors.
1. metaphor
2. metaphor
3. simile
4. metaphor
5. metaphor
6. simile
7. simile
8. simile
9. metaphor
10. simile
11. metaphor
12. metaphor
13. metaphor
14. metaphor
15. simile
16. simile
17. simile
18. metaphor

Warm-Up 108 (page 115)
1. game
2. furniture
3. car
4. well
5. hairless
6. laugh
7. right
8. catch
9. loose
10. sip/drink
11. talk
12. hear/listen

Warm-Up 109 (page 116)
1. hear/listen: function
2. spell: function
3. sky: relationship
4. scrambled/boiled: cause and effect
5. down: antonyms
6. month: part-whole
7. frown: cause and effect
8. arms: part-whole
9. cat: offspring-adult relationship
10. even: function

Check to make sure the student has completed each analogy.

Warm-Up 110 (page 117)
Check to make sure the student has written an appropriate analogy for each category.

Warm-Up 111 (page 118)
1. age, agent, aghast, agony, agriculture, assemble, assignment, asterisk, asteroid, astronaut
2. judge, jumbo, jumping, junction, June, jungle, juniper, junk, Jupiter, juror

3. cheap, chicken, child, chilly, chime, chimney, chintz, chip, chomp, church
4. roast, robot, rocketry, rodeo, Roman, romance, romper, rooster, rosette, royal
5. manager, Manchurian, mandarin, mange, maniac, mannequin, mannerly, mantle, manual, manuscript

Warm-Up 112 (page 119)
Sample answers:
1. Poland–Pot
polar, police, pollinate, polygraph, pomegranate, pompom, pooch, poodle, pork, post
2. Naught–Number
naughty, nautical, newscast, newspaper, newsworthy, noisy, nose, notes, noteworthy, numb
Check to make sure the student has completed the chart.

Warm-Up 113 (page 120)
1. vacuum
2. believe
3. ✔
4. truly
5. dumbbell
6. occasionally
7. grateful
8. embarrass
9. misspell
10. ✔
11. privilege
12. receive
13. rhythm
14. library
Check to make sure the student has written each troublesome word as well as ways of remembering how to spell each troublesome word.

Warm-Up 114 (page 121)
accessory (#2)   regardless (#2)   probably (#2)
dilate (#2)   library (#1)   realtor (#1)
sherbet (#1)   miniature (#1)   escape (#2)
espresso (#1)   height (#2)   February (#2)
utmost (#2)   mischievous (#2)
Check to make sure the student has written other frequently mispronounced words.

Warm-Up 115 (page 122)
Check to make sure the student has completed the Glossary activity page.

Warm-Up 116 (page 123)
Check to make sure the student has written three synonyms for each word.
Sample answers:
1. The **ship** was large and luxurious.
2. A **human** scribbled all over the walls.
3. I want a **mutt** that is fluffy, large, and smart.

Warm-Up 117 (page 124)
Check to make sure the student has written three synonyms for each word.
Check to make sure the student has replaced each underlined word in the sentences with one of the synonyms from the top of the page.

Warm-Up 118 (page 125)
Sample answers:
Paragraph #1
blue uniform/crisp uniform
shines her yellow badge/polishes her gold badge
polishes her shoes/buffs her shoes
the belt contains/the belt's compartments house
clean patrol car/spiffy patrol car
Paragraph #2
the quiet student/the industrious student
read a book/perused a book

the book was good/the book was interesting
he put the book back into his backpack/ he returned the book to his knapsack
the student took out a notebook and pencil/the student took out a spiral notebook and mechanical pencil
Paragraph #3
my dog likes to chew/my dog likes to chomp
my dog likes big bones/my dog likes enormous bones
giant-sized ones/meaty ones

Warm-Up 119 (page 126)
Check to make sure the student has completed the Card Catalog activity page.

Warm-Up 120 (page 127)
Check to make sure the student has completed the Dewey Decimal System activity page.

Warm-Up 121 (page 128)
Check to make sure the student has completed the Dewey Decimal System activity page.

Warm-Up 122 (page 129)
Check to make sure the student has completed the Dewey Decimal System activity page.
1. 550
2. 510
3. 520
4. 530
5. 570

Warm-Up 123 (page 130)
Check to make sure the student has completed the Dewey Decimal System activity page.

Warm-Up 124 (page 131)
1. N
2. M
3. K
4. Q
5. U
6. J
7. C–F
8. T
9. S
10. P
11. L
12. A
13. G
14. G
15. G
16. R
17. S
18. V
19. G
20. N

Warm-Up 125 (page 132)
Check to make sure the student has completed the Periodical Index activity page.

Warm-Up 126 (page 133)
Check to make sure the student has completed the Periodical Index activity page.

Warm-Up 127 (page 134)
Check to make sure the student has completed the Citing Sources activity page.

Warm-Up 128 (page 135)
Check to make sure the student has completed the Citing Sources activity page.

Warm-Up 129 (page 136)
1. There is no such thing as a free puppy: Puppies need vet care, food, toys, and treats.
2. Taking care of your smile is easy: Brush and floss your teeth each day.
3. The tree's bark was scraped, branches were broken, and food was missing: The wild cat had struck again.
4. Everybody must wear the school uniform: shirts, pants, socks, and ties.
5. We made many projects in arts and crafts class: coffee mugs, dinner plates, and vases.
6. I know how Abigail earned an A on her test: She copied Amber.
7. The car was packed with kids, suitcases, snacks, and the family dog: Seattle, here we come!

8. Campers must follow the rules to be safe in the mountains: Clean up trash, put out the campfire, and store food in the metal lockboxes.
9. The food was cold: Mario missed dinner again.
10. In order to get a good night's sleep, Penny has to have her stuffed animals: Sadie, Figaro, Vigo, and Zeta.

Warm-Up 130 (page 137)
Check to make sure the student has underlined and written the following words:
1. *Red and Purple: More Than Just Colors*
2. 10:45 a.m.
3. Chicago: Farm Hands Publishing
4. *How to Boil Water: A Cookbook for Beginners*
5. 11:30 a.m.
6. 10:21B
7. *Mothers: They Are Always There*
8. 11:25X
9. 4:00
10. 3:20
11. Dear Sir:
12. 11:15
13. 25:087
14. *Being Green: Twelve Easy Steps*

Warm-Up 131 (page 138)
1. Christopher is in room six; his twin brother is in room seven.
2. Montel is on television; he anchors the morning news.
3. My dog was barking up a storm; it wanted me to rub its belly.
4. Nancy wants to be a school psychologist; however, her parents want her to be an engineer.
5. The doorbell rang; nobody answered it.
6. The children were naughty with the babysitter; therefore, they had to go to bed early.
7. James finished his report; he gave it to the teacher.
8. Marty carefully folded the towels, sheets, and blankets; cleaned the windows, floors, and baseboards; and straightened the cushions, seat covers, and throw pillows.
9. Bertha learned how to ride a unicycle; still, she is afraid of losing her balance on it.
10. Anne just graduated from nursing school; therefore, she will be looking for a job.
11. Billy practices the piano every day; he plays very well.
12. Stu runs several miles each morning; consequently, he is in great shape.

Warm-Up 132 (page 139)
1. none needed
2. "Turn to page twenty-four in your science books," said Mrs. Plumb.
3. none needed
4. "Stop by the cafeteria, and see our amazing display of student artwork," announced the principal.
5. "It was an accident," said Madge.
6. "Look out!" screamed Nadia.

"Hey, Josh! Let's head over there and get some air time!"
"Sounds good to me," replied Josh.
"I can't wait to try the big ramp!" said Josh.
"Me, too," said Zack. "I have also been wanting to try out the wall."

"Watch this!" screamed Josh.
"Whoa! That was amazing!" said Zack.

Warm-Up 133 (page 140)
For the Peach Blossom Festival, our class read the poem, "Follow the Teacher."
The boys started the poem with, "We were following the teacher/And talking to each other," and then Bryce fell off the stage!
"Bryce, are you okay?" asked Carly. Bryce was a bit woozy and started singing "Wheels on the Bus" but soon forgot the words.
"I am okay," said Bryce, "but maybe we can start the poem over."
"Next time," said Bryce, "I will be more careful about where I am standing."

Warm-Up 134 (page 141)
1. Mary's chair is big.
2. The plane's pilot enjoys flying.
3. Steve's boom box is black.
4. This is Garth's passport.
5. Stan's birthday is next week.

1. doesn't	6. they'd	11. wouldn't	16. hasn't
2. she'll	7. he's	12. I've	17. you're
3. isn't	8. you'll	13. I'm	18. we're
4. don't	9. we've	14. won't	19. couldn't
5. they're	10. could've	15. they'll	20. should've

Warm-Up 135 (page 142)
Check to make sure the student has underlined the following words: familys, Luis, Sandovals, Kates

Kate travels the world looking for unique items for her family's store and for her customers. In Luis' rug store, Kate found the perfect rug for the Sandovals' house.

The colors were beautiful. Luis said that the blue in the rug matched Kate's eyes perfectly.

Check to make sure the student has underlined the following words: Karis, its, ones, doesnt, dont, elses, wont, doctors, wont

Kari's doctor tells people it's easy to avoid getting sick. The doctor says to wash one's hands with soap and water several times each day. Soap doesn't allow germs to multiply and spread. The doctor also says don't drink from someone else's cup. This won't let germs transfer from one person to another. Follow the doctor's advice, and you won't get sick this year.

Warm-Up 136 (page 143)
Check to make sure the student has added a comma to the following sentences:
1. I thought I left my glasses here, but I can't find them.
2. It was time for the play to start, but the cast was not ready to go onstage.
3. Henry was extremely thirsty, so he drank some water.
5. The printer doesn't work, so I called a repairperson.
6. The cable car couldn't stop, so the people jumped out of its way.
7. Paul left his jacket at home, so I let him borrow mine.
8. The telephone was dropped, yet it still works.
9. The lawn needs to be mowed, and the leaves need to be raked.

11. Joan is running for treasurer, for she is good with money. Check to make sure the student has written three sentences with coordinating conjunctions.

Warm-Up 137 (page 144)

Check to make sure the student has added a comma to the following sentences:

1. Because it was out of gas, the car wouldn't start.
2. After the party was over, we all went to Dave's house.
4. After we eat dinner, let's play tag.
5. When you hear the whistle blow, start running.
8. If the grass is dry, it needs more water.
9. As soon as Jim gets here, we can head off to the mountains.
12. Since it is so hot, why don't we all head to the local swimming pool?

Check to make sure the student has written three sentences with dependent clauses.

Warm-Up 138 (page 145)

1. <u>In the middle of the night</u>, the door squeaked open.
2. <u>Crying crankily</u>, the baby finally fell asleep.
3. <u>Well</u>, here comes Mr. Iverson.
4. <u>Meanwhile</u>, we all sat in our seats waiting for the speech to begin.
5. <u>Still</u>, it's about time you started looking for a job.
6. <u>After directing a film</u>, Tabitha McNeery visited our acting company.
7. <u>Furthermore</u>, more students are deciding to go to college than into the work force.
8. <u>Feeling sick</u>, Jan decided not to go to school.
9. <u>Making up his mind</u>, Jeremy ordered a hamburger.
10. <u>To look at houses on the market</u>, Roger called a real estate agent.

Check to make sure the student has written each sentence with an introductory phrase or word.

Warm-Up 139 (page 146)

1. Would you like a glass of lemonade, water, milk, or iced tea?
2. Nina invited Seth, Bob, Ben, Trina, and Maggie to her party.
3. Sam packed shirts, pants, socks, and shoes for his trip to Maine.
4. Katie can't find her purse, wallet, or keys.
5. The Sorensons visited five states: New York, Pennsylvania, New Jersey, Maryland, and Virginia.
6. This semester, Al is taking physics, calculus, poetry, and Spanish.
7. On Saturday, we can go to the water park, the amusement park, or the bowling alley.
8. While camping, we saw squirrels, moose, owls, and bears.

Warm-Up 140 (page 147)

1. Heather, who enjoys reading, edits children's books.
2. Bugsy, whose real name is Bogart, likes to act like he's big and tough.
3. The mug, which is made from glass, is full of hot coffee.

Check to make sure the student has written each sentence with a nonessential clause.

Visalia, California, a small town in the Central Valley, is my hometown. I was born on July 30, 1980, at the local hospital. My mother, after bringing me home from the hospital, could not believe how little I was. She said, "This is the tiniest

baby I have ever seen!" Well, she could not say that for long because I ate and ate and ate and ate!

Warm-Up 141 (page 148)

1. My family spent summer vacation in Orlando, Florida.
2. Trina and Betty are best friends.
3. Have you ever eaten at Daisy's Restaurant?
4. We went back-to-school shopping at Bennet's Department Store.
5. Which case went to the Supreme Court?
6. Clay gave a wonderful speech about honesty.
7. My car, the red Viva, gets wonderful gas mileage.
8. My parakeets, Bailey and Luna, love to take baths.

Warm-Up 142 (page 149)

Check to make sure the student has underlined and written the following words:

1. Let's
2. Did, Coach Henson
3. Grandma, Grandpa, Exeter
4. Learning, Love, School
5. Judge Alexander
6. Uncle Bill, Austin, Texas
7. My
8. The, Times, Make, Best
9. Sergeant Evans
10. The, Time, It ,Takes, Listen
11. The
12. My, Professor Marx

Warm-Up 143 (page 150)

Check to make sure the student has underlined and written the following words:

1. Fridays, Sundays
2. February
3. West Orange County
4. Labor Day, September
5. June, July, August
6. Pacific Northwest
7. Mother's Day, May
8. Mondays
9. South Chicago
10. Independence Day

Check to make sure the student has answered each question using a complete sentence.

Warm-Up 144 (page 151)

Check to make sure the student has answered each question.

1. My favorite football team, the Exeter Crawdads, is playing at the Lemon Bowl.
2. The Democratic Convention is being held next week.
3. My sisters and I are members of the Girl Scouts.
4. I love the music that is played at Padre games.
5. Do you know how to speak Mandarin or Cantonese?
6. My dad has been to Germany, France, and England.
7. Green Peace is an organization that works to protect our environment.
8. Tiny Foxtail is a Native American.

Warm-Up 145 (page 152)

Check to make sure the student has completed the chart.

Check to make sure the student has underlined and written the following words on the lines: J.J., Renaissance, Ottoman Empire, Starbucks®, J.J.

Warm-Up 146 (page 153)

Check to make sure the student has underlined and written the following words:

1. disport=sport
2. mathematics=math
3. caravan=van
4. pantaloons=pants
5. fanatic=fan
6. autobus=bus

7. pianoforte=piano
8. advertisement=ad
9. zoological gardens=zoo
10. influenza=flu
11. examination=exam
12. microphone=mic
13. of the clock=o'clock
14. cinematograph=cinema
16. periwig=wig

Warm-Up 147 (page 154)

1. brunch
2. cheeseburger
3. moped
4. paratroops
5. smog
6. telethon
7. twirl
8. travelogue
9. glimmer
10. motel
11. motocross
12. splatter
13. pixel
14. flare
15. flurry
16. clash
17. slosh
18. bit

1. bash/bang + smash
2. Bollywood/Bombay + Hollywood
3. cyborg/cybernetic + organism
4. sporks/spoons + forks
5. dumbfounded/dumb + confounded

Warm-Up 148 (page 155)

1. greif/grief
2. no misspelled words
3. recieved/received
4. feirce/fierce
5. peirce/pierce
6. reciepts/receipts
7. nieghs/neighs
8. no misspelled words
9. decieve/deceive
10. cieling/ceiling
11. frieght/freight
12. beleive/believe

Warm-Up 149 (page 156)

1. cedar
2. Celsius
3. civil
4. guitar
5. carnivore
6. gerbil
7. guest
8. cat
9. guess
10. costume
11. receipt
12. peace
13. guppy
14. cab

Warm-Up 150 (page 157)

1. duck
2. sneak
3. shook
4. sink
5. oak
6. picnic
7. arithmetic
8. clock
9. knock
10. thank
11. bunk
12. blink
13. elastic
14. pack
15. music
16. antibiotics

Warm-Up 151 (page 158)

1. cactus
2. cake
3. calendar
4. kilt
5. calf
6. California
7. kite
8. curly
9. cup
10. kick
11. Canada
12. kitchen
13. key
14. coconut
15. ketchup
16. king

Warm-Up 152 (page 159)

1. launch
2. butcher
3. fetch/catch
4. teach
5. search
6. ditch
7. ketchup
8. pitcher
9. pinched
10. itch
11. scratch
12. match
13. sketch
14. bench

Check to make sure the student has written three words to fit each spelling rule.

Warm-Up 153 (page 160)

1. BASIC
2. RADAR
3. NATO
4. RIF
5. NOW
6. FIAT
7. ROM
8. LASER
9. ZIP
10. GASP
11. SONAR
12. ASAP
13. FEAR
14. HAZMAT
15. PIN
16. TIPS
17. SWAT
18. DEW Line
19. TEAM
20. NASA

Warm-Up 154 (page 161)

1. VIP
2. RV
3. UFO
4. RPM
5. CPA
6. MLK
7. PI
8. NIB
9. TLC
10. TGIF
11. ET
12. PA
13. FYI
14. ID
15. AKA
16. MYOB
17. PS
18. BLT
19. AC
20. IQ

Warm-Up 155 (page 162)

1. jeannine, tim
2. table^
3. dad
4. cards ~~our~~ are, friday
5. ~~Jan.~~ January (so)
6. skidded,^ flipped over,^ and spilled
7. Don'^t, zoo,^ and don't
8. dora
9. i ,work^
10. david's snow shop
11. Chicago,^ Illinois
12. ~~n.~~ north (so), ~~e.~~ east (so)

Warm-Up 156 (page 163)

June 22, 2009

To whom it may concern:

I am writing to you about one of your products. i recently (sp) purchased one of your pens, the Super gel Writer. I ~~thunk~~ think (sp) the Super Gel Writer is one of the best pens on the market. It ~~write~~ writes (sp) so smoothly^ and the ink doesn'^t smudge. This is so important because I am left-^handed. With some pens, the ink dries so ~~slow~~ slowly (sp) that ~~us~~ we (sp) lefties end up smearing it all over the paper when we write. And we lefties are then stuck walking around with ink stains on ^our hands or, even worse, on ^clothes! Thank ~~u~~ you (sp) for this ~~grate~~ great (sp) product!

our

~~You're~~ Your (sp) faithful customer,

I. M. Writer